PIE
of the day

Peter Russell-Clarke

Lothian
BOOKS

Thomas C. Lothian Pty Ltd
11 Munro Street, Port Melbourne, Victoria 3207

Copyright text and illustrations © Peter Russell-Clarke 1998
First published 1998

All rights reserved. No part of this publication may be reproduced, stored in a retrieval system or transmitted in any form by any means without the prior permission of the copyright owner. Enquiries should be made to the publisher.

National Library of Australia
Cataloguing-in-Publication data:

Russell-Clarke, Peter,
 Pie of the day.

 Includes index.
 ISBN 0 85091 882 0.

 1. Pies. I. Title.

641.8652

Designed by Ogden Art and Design
Typeset in 9.5 pt Leawood Book by Ogden Art and Design
Printed in Australia by Robertson Printing Pty Ltd

CONTENTS

1	**Introduction**	40	Corned beef pie No. 2
3	A pie by any other name	41	Budget pie
		42	Budget pie No. 1
7	**The basics**	43	Budget pie No. 2
8	Shortcrust pastry	44	Shepherd's pie
9	Sweet shortcrust pastry		
10	Puff pastry	45	**Lamb, pork, veal and rabbit pies**
12	Hot-water crust pastry		
14	Hints on pastry making	45	Danny's pie
15	Equipment	49	Lamb pie with forcemeat balls
17	Simple Simon	51	Large meat pie with filo pastry
19	**Beef pies**	52	Chinese meat pie
19	Minced beef pie	53	Raised pork pie
21	Steak and egg pie	56	Loin of pork cooked in pastry
22	Tomato sauce		
23	My own steak and oyster pie	57	Bacon, spinach and tomato pasta pie
24	Tamale pie		
25	Ally Oop's flat pie	59	Pompous pie
28	Beef and mushroom loaf in pastry	63	Rabbit pie
29	Sausage rolls are pies in disguise	65	**Chicken pies**
		65	Skinny
30	Sausage rolls with tomato or avocado sauce	67	Chicken pie
		69	The night father stuck his head in the oven
33	An Aussie in Paris		
35	Steak and kidney pie	72	Deep dish chicken pie with mushrooms
37	A corned beef and cabbage story		
		73	Peter's stuffed chicken breasts in rice paper
38	Corned beef pie No. 1		

iii

CONTENTS

75 Fish pies
75 The Admiral, the 'pinkers' and the pie
79 Eel pie
80 Fish pie
81 Fresh oyster tart
83 Perc's pie

87 Pies with egg
87 Egg and bacon pie (quiche)
88 Spinach pie
89 Cauliflower, carrot and Parmesan quiche
90 Quick crust quiche
91 Onion pie
92 Peter's crunchy rice pie

93 Vegetarian pies
93 Television debut
95 Four different cheese pies
97 Pumpkin
99 Sour cream–pumpkin pie
100 My son's jumbo vegetable rolls
101 Chick pea pies
103 Leek and goat cheese tarts
104 Potatoes in a pastry shell
105 My Dad's vegetable pasties
106 Pasties with vegetable coulis
107 Baked beans

109 Pizza pies
109 Cheesy ideas
113 No cheese please
116 Tuscan pizza
117 Potato pizza
118 Chilli mini pizzas
119 Vegetarian pizza
120 Pizza sandwich
121 Crusty pizza
122 Three-corner pizza

123 Thai pies
123 The mysterious curry puff
124 How to assemble and cook a curry puff
124 Classic puff filling
124 Variations: Nos 1–17

131 Festive pies
131 Emu pie
133 Individual emu pie
135 Pâté of goose or duck with a crust
136 Crusted turkey pie
137 Rising sun
139 Pigeon pie (from Queen Victoria's chef)
140 Quail and caviar tarts

141 Sweet pies
141 Pear pie
142 Mince pie
143 Jackson pie
144 Glacé citrus pie
145 Lime tart
147 Lemon cream cheese pie
148 Pecan pie
149 Custard tarts
150 Rhubarb pie
151 Old-fashioned apple pie
152 The last crust

155 Index

Introduction

G'day,

Run rabbit, run rabbit, run, run, run
Don't give the farmer his fun, fun, fun.
He'll get by without his rabbit pie,
So run rabbit, run rabbit, run, run, run.

The good old rabbit pie was a traditional favourite with country folk. Alas it has fallen out of favour, and it looks as if the calicivirus means that we shall all have to forego the underground mutton pie. Dear reader, take heart, there are other fabulous pie fillings which history and I have concocted that are sure to find a place in your heart as well as your tummy.

My marvellous but long departed mum was a pie-ophile. All and everything from the coolgardie would be diced and cooked under her flaky pastry.

I lived much of my early life in Tumut, a small country town at the south end of the Snowy Mountains. My mother was the district's dressmaker. We lived in the back of her shop which was opposite the Tumut Hotel in Russell Street. Mrs Tuttie, the pub's cook, was a huge woman with forearms that rivalled a haunch of ham and a tummy the size of a World War II barrage balloon. Her generosity and all-embracing goodwill were as famous as her pub pies.

Unlike most butchers and cooks she never minced her mutton. 'It squeezes out the moisture and, after all, that's the flavour,' she'd boom. 'You cut it up with a very sharp knife,' which she proceeded to wield to underline her point.

INTRODUCTION

Mrs Tuttie made her own pastry, grew her own herbs and vegetables, ran her own sheep, chopped her own wood, lit her own stove, as well as ate her own pies.

'How else would you know whether they're any good?' she'd roar, tears of laughter streaming down her ample cheeks.

Not only did the drunks of Tumut know her pies were perfect, but she also taught my whole family to cook. And many of the recipes in this tome are a tribute to her cooking abilities as well as my mum's staying power . . . you see, Mrs Tuttie drank many a big beer as she imparted her knowledge.

A pie by any other name

In my more mundane moments I think of a pie simply as a football day accessory — a snack enriched with a spurt of dead horse — the discarded crust ferociously fought over by football-following seagulls.

It is often a grey slurry of unidentifiable origin contained in a crumbling cocoon of plaster, yet somehow still dear to those hardy Australians who brave the elements to cheer a pig's bladder being booted about by desperate men.

Our meat pie, the symbol of Australia.

Yet my dictionary informs me a 'pie' is also the word used to describe a gossip or even an Indian copper coin. The word 'pie' describes objects or beings having elements which are dissimilar, such as a piebald horse. Piebald actually describes any animal with a white spot on its face or, like a magpie, a white flash on its body. The other colour (if one can describe white as a colour) need not be black. No sir. It can be any darker colour or even various colours.

Having a finger in the pie is what the in-laws are adept at and it is written that promises, like pie crusts, are made to be broken.

Π^2 has nothing to do with Greek pies, nor does pie-eyed, though the serving of pies at pubs could cause the consumption of more alcohol than one can cope with comfortably.

So you see 'pie' is ever-present in all sorts of shapes and sizes.

Usually a pie is a dish of meat, fish, fruit, vegetables or just about any other food covered with a crust and baked. Most of us under-

A pie by any other name

stand the crust to be a pastry yet Shepherd's Pie has a beret of mashed potatoes. Pies can also be covered with crusts of bread, biscuits or cake crumbs or even whipped egg whites as in a Lemon Meringue Pie.

A pastry shell without a crust or lid is usually known as a tart or a flan, but Americans still call them pies. For instance, we all know of their traditional Pumpkin Pie.

But there are all sorts of other pies as well. A raised pie is moulded from hot-water pastry with its own top, base and walls of pastry. A flat square of pastry can have its corners folded in to enclose the meat, poultry and other contents which make up the filling and it is called an envelope pie or, more strictly, a pasty, and that's another story altogether. Or you can have unbaked pies known as refrigerator pies, which are simply a pie shell of crumbs with a chocolate or butter base, set firm in the refrigerator and then filled with ice-cream or cream and fruit mixtures.

A pie by any other name

Italy's famous pizza would, if it was made in England, be called a Savoury Flan. But pizza, as we Aussie intellectuals know, simply means Pie.

Now, to add further to your knowledge, early in the Middle Ages, around the 10th to 14th century, the Pommie pie often mixed both savoury and sweet ingredients such as minced pork and apple sauce. But since then it has been either one or the other. Both the Savoury Meat Pie we spill down our shirts or blouses at the footy, and the Mince Pie at Christmas time, which is filled with semi-dried and candied fruits, is a pie to us. Of course, in far-off countries there are far more exotic names for these tasty flaky morsels. But whatever nomenclature we use, we Aussies expect a *pâté en croûté* to taste terrific. I'm sure you'll enjoy the flavours we have put together from my own kitchen or I've pinched from even more salubrious establishments.

The basics

Pastry is simply a paste of fat and flour with water added to make a dough for shaping and baking. Pastry-making is a century-old art, certainly known to the Ancient Greeks and Romans, though its major development in the western world dates from the late eighteenth century.

The flour used today is normally plain wheaten, but it may be replaced or supplemented by other flours or admixtures of things such as mashed potato. It may have baking powder, yeast or other leaveners. Butter remains the favourite fat but good results are also achieved with vegetable oils.

All pastries call for maximum convenient coolness in the ingredients, minimum handling of the dough and, at least to start with, a very hot oven.

Most recipes call for a little salt to be sifted with the flour.

All liquids should be added carefully lest the dough becomes sticky and unmanageable.

The most commonly used pastes are short (shortcrust, flan, cheese pastry and suet crust) or flaked (puff, rough puff and flaky).

THE BASICS

Shortcrust pastry

Shortcrust pastry is made with 4 parts flour to 2 parts fat. It should have a crisp, short (melt-in-the-mouth) texture. This is achieved by rubbing the fat and flour together with your fingers to make a crumb-like mixture with an even distribution of fat-coated particles.

The pastry is usually baked at 190–220°C (375–425°F). See 'To Blind Bake' page 15.

Ingredients

225 g (7 oz) plain flour

½ teaspoon salt

50 g (1½ oz) lard*

50 g (1½ oz) butter

2 tablespoons cold water

* use butter if lard is not available

Method

Sieve the flour and salt into a bowl. Cut the fat into 1.5 cm (½") cubes and distribute evenly over the flour.

Rub the fat lightly into the flour with your fingertips, lifting up the mixture while rubbing to keep it as cool and airy as possible. Continue rubbing until the mixture resembles fine breadcrumbs.

Make a well in the centre of the mixture and add the water gradually while you stir it in with a knife. Use just enough water to produce a soft (not sticky) dough.

Turn out the dough onto a floured surface and roll it (once only) to the thickness required. The pastry will be heavy if you roll it too much.

This recipe makes **one quantity** of shortcrust pastry; enough to line and cover a 23 cm (9") pie plate. For a slightly larger dish size, roll out the pastry a little thinner.

Sweet shortcrust pastry

Flans and tarts that are served cold are sometimes made with sweet, enriched shortcrust pastry that can be rolled out very thinly.

Ingredients

225 g (7 oz) plain flour

½ teaspoon salt

125 g (4 oz) butter

1 tablespoon caster sugar

2 egg yolks

1 tablespoon cold water

Method

Prepare the flour and mix in the butter as for shortcrust pastry.

Then add the sugar and mix it in well.

Beat the egg yolks together and mix in the cold water. Make a well in the centre of the flour and stir in the egg and water mixture with a knife to produce a soft dough.

Turn out the dough onto a floured board and knead gently until it is pliable and free of cracks.

Roll it out once to the required thickness.

The pastry is usually baked at 190–220°C (375–425°F). See 'To Blind Bake' page 15.

THE BASICS

Puff pastry (sometimes called Flaky pastry)

This pastry has thin crisp layers with air in between. It is made with 4 parts flour to 3 parts fat and is particularly suitable for pies that are served cold.

The flaky texture is achieved by kneading lightly then folding and rolling the dough in layers with dabs of fat between. The dabs of fat produce air pockets and help to separate the flakes.

When the pastry is baked at a high temperature, steam rises between the flaked layers and lifts them. It is usually baked at 220°C (425°F).

Ingredients

225 g (7 oz) plain flour

½ teaspoon salt

175 g (6 oz) firm butter

1 teaspoon lemon juice

100–125 ml (3–4 fl oz) cold water

Method

Sieve the flour and salt into a bowl.

Divide the butter into four equal portions.

Take one portion of butter and cut it into small pieces. Rub it into the flour with your fingertips, lifting up the mixture while rubbing to keep it as cool and airy as possible. Continue until the mixture resembles fine breadcrumbs.

Make a well in the centre of the mixture. Add the lemon juice and just enough water to form a firm elastic dough. Mix together with a knife.

Turn out the dough onto a floured board and knead it until it is free of cracks.

Roll the dough into a strip three times as long as it is wide and about 2.5 cm (1") thick.

Take a second portion of the butter and, with a knife, flake it in even rows along →

THE BASICS

two-thirds of the strip of pastry. Leave a clear strip about 2.5 cm (1") wide along the edge of the pastry strip. If the butter is too close to the edge it will be squeezed out when you roll the pastry.

Fold one-third of the strip (the end with no butter) over to the middle. Then fold the other end (covered with butter) over that, so that the pastry is folded into three layers.

Turn the pastry around so that an open edge is towards you, then leave it to relax for 15–20 minutes in a cool place.

Press the open edges together with a rolling pin to enclose the air. Then make ridges in two or three places by pressing with the rolling pin. This distributes the air and stops it from collecting in one large bubble that is difficult not to break when rolling.

Roll out the pastry again to a strip three times as long as its width, then flake on the third portion of butter in the same way as the second. Fold, rest, seal and ridge as before.

Repeat the whole process using the fourth portion of butter. Then roll out to the thickness required.

This recipe makes **one quantity** of pastry; enough for a base and lid for a 23 cm (9") pie plate. For a slightly larger dish, roll out the pastry a little thinner.

THE BASICS

Hot-water crust pastry

Hot-water crust pastry or 'raised' pastry is similar in texture to shortcrust, but the dough is stiff enough to be 'raised' — that is, to stand alone without the support of a dish. It is made with 3 or 4 parts flour to 1 part fat and mixed with boiling liquid. The pastry is usually used for pork, game, or veal and ham pies. It is usually cooked at a high temperature at 200°C (400°F) for 20–30 minutes, then at a lower temperature at 100°C (200°F) a while longer, depending on the pie ingredients.

Ingredients

225 g (7 oz) plain flour

½ teaspoon salt

50 g (1½ oz) lard*

100–125 ml (3–4 fl oz) liquid (equal quantities of milk and water)

* use butter if lard is not available

Method

Prepare the filling before making the pastry.

Warm a pastry board, bowl, wooden spoon and the mould you will be using (see below).

Sieve the flour and salt into the warmed bowl and make a well in the middle of the flour. Put the fat and liquid into a saucepan, bring to the boil, then pour at once into the flour well.

Mix rapidly with a wooden spoon to a soft, elastic dough.

Turn out onto a floured board and knead until smooth. If the pastry is too dry, add a few drops of boiling water.

Cut off one-third of the pastry to make the lid, and keep it warm and moist by placing it in a container over a bowl of hot water while you are moulding the case.

Mould the pastry case into the required

THE BASICS

shape while it is still warm, otherwise it will become too hard and difficult to handle. There are four ways of moulding:

- *Over a floured jar or tin.*
- *By joining a strip for the side and two circles for the base and lid.*
- *Moulding the shape with your hands.*
- *Lining a special mould which has hinged sides and a detachable base.*

Place a double strip of greaseproof paper, secured with a piece of string, around each moulded pie. Scoop the pre-prepared filling into the case. Put the lid on the case squeezing the edges together. Make two holes in the lid to allow steam to escape. Leave the greaseproof paper on the case for the first 20 minutes of cooking.

After baking, allow the pie to cool before pouring in stock through a funnel inserted in the steam vents. Good stock forms a jelly as it cools.

This recipe makes enough pastry for a 20 cm (8") pie dish or four small pies.

THE BASICS

Hints on pastry making

When mixing and rolling pastry, the aim is to introduce as much air as possible so that the pastry will rise well when heated. The colder the air, the more it will expand when heated during cooking.

Keep all utensils and ingredients as cool as possible, and wash your hands in cold water before you mix pastry. The only exception to this is when making hot-water crust pastry.

Rolling pastry

If time allows, leave the lump of pastry to rest in a cool place for 10–20 minutes before rolling it out (unless it contains baking powder). Resting the pastry is especially important in hot weather. Pastry that gets over-heated during handling will be tough.

Dredge the board and rolling pin with flour, but not the pastry. Too much flour rolled in can alter the ratio of flour to fat, particularly if you are making only a small quantity.

When rolling pastry use short, quick, light strokes with even pressure from both hands. Always roll in a forward direction and lift the pin between strokes. Stop rolling just short of the edges to ensure a uniform thickness and to avoid squeezing out air. Lift the pastry at the edges to make sure it isn't sticking to the board. If it is, very lightly dust beneath it with flour.

Don't handle pastry unless necessary. To move it, or lift it onto a dish, turn it over a floured rolling pin. Unroll it onto a freshly dredged surface or across the surface of the dish. The rolled side of the pastry is the smoothest and should be used for the pie surface.

Storing uncooked pastry

All pastry can be stored after mixing until ready for use except for pastry which contains baking powder. If sealed in a polythene bag, the pastry will keep in the fridge for up to 3 days, whether in a lump or rolled and shaped. It can also be deep frozen for up to 3 months, but roll and shape it before freezing.

Shortcrust pastry, mixed to a crumb stage but with no liquid added, can be stored in a polythene bag or covered container in the

THE BASICS

fridge for up to 4 weeks. It can also be deep frozen for up to 6 months.

To blind bake

A pastry case is baked blind — without a filling — if the filling needs little or no cooking or will be added later. Shortcrust pastry, plain or sweet, is the only type of pastry appropriate for blind baking.

Line a pie dish with homemade or ready-made pastry. Prick the base of the pastry lining with a fork to let the air out.

Cover the base with a circle of greaseproof paper or foil and put in a temporary filling of dried beans or rice to prevent the pastry rising.

Bake in the centre of a pre-heated oven at 190°C (375°F) for about 15 minutes. When the pastry is cooked, take out the greaseproof paper or foil and the filling and put the case back into the oven for 2–3 minutes to dry out.

Equipment

One of the great pleasures of cooking is to have superb equipment. One of the trials of cooking is inadequate equipment. For instance, it's a joy to use a well-balanced knife which maintains a keen edge and looks business-like. The steel of the blade needs to continue through the handle which needs to be shaped for a secure grip. There's no fun in using a cheap steak knife.

As knives vary in quality, so do pie dishes. Cheap tin dishes have a tendency to warp and rust. I have cast iron dishes encased in enamel but I also like glazed pottery. The shape, size and design is, of course, a personal choice.

I use a marble pastry board because it remains cool. I'm also attracted to the look and feel of marble. Nevertheless there are some excellent plastic pastry boards on the market.

I have a selection of wooden, marble and glass rolling pins, both fancy and plain, some with ball-bearings in the handle which allow control and a feel for what you are doing.

THE BASICS

For my pots and pans I prefer stainless steel with copper bottoms to cast iron simply because cast iron pots can be extremely heavy, especially laden with food.

I'm not one for gadgetry because it clutters the kitchen cupboards and work space.

A good serving spoon is essential though, as is a wooden spoon and spatula, as well as a serving spoon with drain holes in it and a colander, both made of stainless steel. A stainless steel egg whisk and a copper bowl for whisking eggs have earned a place in my kitchen too.

I don't use oven gloves; a kitchen towel doubled is sufficient.

You could list aprons and flan dishes, egg cups and coddlers, food processors and blenders — the list would be almost endless — but I think it's fun to shop and find your own equipment and add to it as you go.

My message is simple. Buy good gear. This doesn't necessarily mean expensive. Cooking should be simple and direct. It should be in good taste and look good, and this is the right recipe for your cooking equipment too!

Dishes for pies

- pie plate
- deep casserole dish
- shallow ovenproof glass dish
- enamel dish
- souffle dish
- quiche or flan dish
- deep muffin tin
- spring form (may have removable base)
- ramekins
- loaf tin
- flat baking tray for pastry puffs and pasties

Simple Simon

> Simple Simon met a pieman
> Going to the fair
> Said Simple Simon to the pieman
> Let me taste your ware
> Said the pieman to Simple Simon
> Show me first your penny
> Said Simple Simon to the pieman
> Alas, I have not any.

Presumably poor old Simple went without his supper. That is, of course, unless the pieman's heart softened.

I met such a softie some years ago when I called on the imposing premises of Four 'n Twenty Pies. They are the Victorian company which, supposedly, baked blackbirds in their pastry before that dainty dish was set before a King. It would seem the RSPCA has nobbled the practice and so the company has looked elsewhere for ingredients!

'Beef is what we bake in our pies,' Ralph Johnson, who was king of the company, smiled at me. 'But the pastry is our secret,' he said. 'I insist on it having a flaky consistency and a buttery taste. Of course it must be strong enough to support the filling, yet soft enough to tempt the most gentle lips. The filling must not be too chunky, nor must it be a slurry. Gristle is a definite no-no, although without the right distribution it doesn't matter whether you've got the recipe right or not.'

I asked to taste his ware and was not asked for a penny or maybe he knew, alas, I had not any. His request was that I film

Simple Simon

what he insisted was a bloody good pie. So I got my meal and some money as well.

I've remained friends with Ralph Johnson who has since retired from pie production to do mysterious deals in China.

All the points posed by Ralph are valid. A pastry must be flaky, buttery, able to support the filling yet not rubbery (see 'Puff pastry' page 10). The filling should not consist of huge hunks of meat nor should it be a thick soup. The bite-sized filling should be coated with a sauce that clings to it. And Ralph was right. The distribution must be carefully orchestrated.

To achieve that aim it is essential that your timing is carefully considered. It is no good serving a piping hot pie when half the people invited to share it are not seated at the table, ready and waiting. It is no good having them wandering around, drink in hand, amiably chatting about friends or the footy because, as I'm sure we've all experienced, once the call of 'Come and get it' is sung, someone wants to go to the toilet, or has to finish their story, or both.

Flaky pastry is so because of heat expanding air trapped between its layers. Once the air cools, the pastry collapses. So, for it to be at its best it needs to be whisked from the oven to the table.

Beef pies

Minced beef pie Serves 4–6

Ingredients

1 onion, chopped

30 g (1 oz) butter

500 g (1 lb) minced beef

2 cups beef stock

1 teaspoon salt

freshly ground black pepper

½ teaspoon mixed dried herbs

2 tablespoons chopped parsley

a pinch of nutmeg

1 tablespoon Worcestershire Sauce

2 tablespoons plain flour

1 quantity shortcrust pastry (see page 8)

Method

Sauté the onion in butter in a heavy saucepan. Cook until soft.

Increase heat and add minced beef. Cook until the meat begins to brown. Drain off excess fat.

Add stock and stir thoroughly. Add seasoning, herbs, parsley, nutmeg and Worcestershire Sauce. Cover saucepan and simmer gently for 30 minutes.

Thicken mince with the flour blended to a smooth paste with a little cold water. Simmer gently for a few minutes until mixture thickens, then cool.

Take two-thirds of the pastry and roll out to fit a round buttered pie plate about 23 cm (9") in diameter (a smaller but deeper dish can be used).

Place the cool minced beef into the pie plate and moisten the pastry edge. Roll out the remainder of the pastry and place it on top of the pie.

Press the edges firmly to seal and trim with a knife. Decorate the edge by fluting it with your fingertips. Make some pastry shapes for the top of the pie. →

BEEF PIES

Brush with beaten egg and bake in oven at 220°C (425°F) for 15 minutes, then reduce the temperature to 180°C (350°F) and bake for a further 25–30 minutes until the pastry is golden brown.

Steak and egg pie Serves 4

Ingredients

12 eyes of bacon rashers

1 kg (2 lb) good quality lean steak

4 small onions, chopped

1 tablespoon olive oil

2 cloves garlic, crushed

freshly ground black pepper

½ teaspoon cumin

1 tablespoon tomato sauce

splash of Worcestershire Sauce

4 drops Tabasco Sauce

4 hard-boiled eggs

1 quantity puff pastry (see page 10) or 4 sheets ready-made pastry

1 egg, beaten

poppyseeds

Method

Cut the bacon into strips and the steak into 2.5 cm (1") cubes.

Heat the oil in a large pan and then put in the onion, bacon, steak, garlic, cumin and black pepper. Sauté these gently over a medium heat for about 5 minutes. Pop in the tomato, Worcestershire and Tabasco sauces and stir them around well.

Take the pan off the heat and then divide the mixture equally into 4 × 11–cm (4½") pie dishes. Slice the hard-boiled eggs and put one egg on top of each pie.

Now, cover each pie dish with the pastry, leaving about a 2.5 cm (1") overhang all around the dish. The pastry, by the way, should be about 3 mm (⅛") thick. Tuck the overhang under the lip of the pie dish or just let it hang down as I often do. Make a little pastry shape to decorate the top.

Brush the pastry over with beaten egg, sprinkle with poppyseeds and then bake it in the oven at 230°C (450°F) until the pastry is golden brown. That'll take 25–30 minutes.

BEEF PIES

Tomato sauce

Ingredients

2 tablespoons olive oil

1 white onion, chopped

500 g (1 lb) ripe tomatoes, skinned and chopped

2 cloves garlic, crushed

freshly ground black pepper

2 tablespoons chopped parsley

¼ cup orange juice

1 teaspoon dried marjoram leaves

Method

Heat the oil in a large heavy pan. Throw in the onion and cook it until it's soft.

Skin the tomatoes by holding them on a fork over a flame or dropping them into very hot water until the skin pops and you can peel it off. Then chop the tomatoes and pop them into the pan as well.

Add the garlic, some freshly ground black pepper, parsley, orange juice and marjoram. Stir it around and then pop the mixture into a blender.

Purée it and then pour it back into the pan. It's too sloppy at this stage for a pie, so turn up the heat and reduce it. This means you bubble out all the water to thicken the sauce.

When it's nice and thick, pour it into a jar with a tight screw top and keep it in your fridge until you're ready to use it. The sauce will keep for about a week depending on how many pies are consumed in the meantime!

BEEF PIES

My own steak and oyster pie Serves 6–8

Ingredients

1 onion, finely sliced

splash of olive oil

1 kg (2 lb) minced steak

100 g (3½ oz) whole button mushrooms

2 tablespoons flour

1 cup beef stock

1 teaspoon Worcestershire Sauce

2 tablespoons tomato paste

1 carrot, finely diced

105 g (3½ oz) smoked oysters, drained

250 g (8 oz) potatoes, peeled, cooked and mashed

1 tablespoon butter

1½ cups grated tasty cheese

1 cup cooked mashed pumpkin

2 tablespoons finely chopped parsley

Method

Cook the onion in a little oil until soft. Add mince and mushrooms, cooking until meat browns. Drain off excess fat.

Add the flour and cook, stirring for a further 2 minutes, then stir in the stock, sauce and tomato paste. Cook until mixture boils and thickens.

Add the carrot and oysters. Spoon meat mixture into an ovenproof dish.

Combine the potatoes, butter and cheese. Add the pumpkin to one-third of the potato mixture and the parsley to the remaining two-thirds. Spoon the two mixtures in alternate spoonful on top of the meat.

Cook at 200°C (400°F) for about 15 minutes, or until the potato has a crust. Keep checking it and remove when brown.

BEEF PIES

Tamale pie Serves 4–6

Ingredients

2 tablespoons butter

500 g (1 lb) lean minced beef

1 onion, chopped

420 g (14 oz) whole kernel corn, undrained

420 g (14 oz) tomatoes, drained

1 cup cultured sour cream

1 cup polenta

⅓ cup black olives, pitted and sliced

1 tablespoon chilli powder

2 teaspoons salt

½ teaspoon cumin

2 cups grated Cheddar cheese

chilli salsa

Method

Melt butter in a large frying pan over medium heat. Add beef and onion and cook for about 4–5 minutes until the meat is lightly browned. Drain off excess fat.

Stir in the corn, tomatoes, sour cream, polenta, olives, chilli powder, salt and cumin. Mix thoroughly.

Sprinkle cheese over the top to within 2.5 cm (1") of the edge. Cover, reduce heat and simmer 20 minutes.

Serve hot with salsa.

Ally Oop's flat pie

Over half a million years ago, our ancestor Ally Oop and his cavemen mates built their kitchens at the mouth of their caves.

They had invented fire, or perhaps it had been invented for them by lightning setting aflame the odd paddock or two. Anyway, we know that back in the dim dark days of the dinosaurs, fire was around.

In fact, archaeologists have unearthed ancient barbecue areas where our culinary-minded ancestors barbecued haunches from their latest hunt.

I'm aware that you might not find this riveting reading, but did you know that these chefs of half a million years ago not only barbecued but also sliced their meat? To date we have been told they ate huge hunks of meat torn from a carcase and eaten raw. Or, once fire was developed, they cooked massive lumps of meat which they tore apart with their strong hands — this was later faithfully copied by that gluttonous king of England, Henry VIII. But now we know that, in those days of yore, Ally Oop had stone knives and ate slivers of meat which he made into pies.

Yes, dear reader, believe me. Ally Oop and his mates heated large smooth rocks in the coals of their fires, smeared them with animal fat, then ground grass seeds, along with seeds and nuts from bushes and shrubs, to make a fine flour. This milled mixture was then mixed with water or milk from a mammoth to make a pastry which was thrown on the rock wet with the animal fat. Slivers of meat and no doubt leaves and grasses were placed on

Ally Oop's flat pie

top of the pastry. The whole lot was covered with another sheet of pastry. After a minute or two this would be turned and the flat pie cooked to perfection.

So it's true pies have been about since well before those ubiquitous blackbirds found themselves in their dainty dish set before the king. Mind you, the pastry would have been better served if it was cooked in an oven, which is what I'm suggesting you do if you follow the following!

BEEF PIES

Ally Oop's Flat Pie Serves 4–6

Ingredients

2 sheets ready-made puff pastry (or 1 quantity of puff pastry, page 10)

1 leg of raw Tyrannosaurus (or approximately 500 g (1 lb) of uncooked beef, lamb, chicken, turkey, ostrich, emu or pork)

½ bunch spinach leaves, blanched

mustard seeds (crack them under the blade of a knife)

garlic salt

6–8 thin slices of skinned eggplant

3 medium tomatoes, skinned and thinly sliced

3 hard-boiled eggs, sliced

1 extra egg, beaten

poppyseeds

Method

Take a sheet of puff pastry sized to suit yourself. Lay very thin slivers of Tyrannosaurus on the pastry. If none is available, you can substitute as desired. Remember, emu and pork have a tendency to dry as they are not fat saturated (therefore brush them with olive oil). Fish would also be fabulous. Everything must be sliced extremely thinly.

Lay some blanched spinach leaves on top of the flesh, some cracked mustard seeds, a sprinkling of garlic salt, thin slices of eggplant and tomato, both of which you've skinned. Now top that with equally thin slices of hard-boiled egg.

Cover the lot with a second sheet of pastry and brush that with a beaten egg. Press the edges together after wetting them with water or the remains of the beaten egg. Sprinkle it with poppyseeds and pop this rather flat pie into the oven, at 230°C (450°F) for 15–20 minutes. When it's golden brown, take it to the table and serve it with a crisp salad.

BEEF PIES

Beef and mushroom loaf in pastry Serves 6–8

Ingredients

1 cup finely chopped button mushrooms

750 g (1½ lb) lean minced steak

2 onions, finely chopped

1 small green capsicum, finely chopped

½ cup tomato paste

¼ cup dried oregano

½ cup grated Parmesan cheese

1 tablespoon garlic salt

1¼ cups fresh breadcrumbs

1 egg, lightly beaten

freshly ground black pepper

375 g (12 oz) ready-made puff pastry (or 1½ quantity puff pastry, see page 10)

Method

Combine all ingredients except pastry. Mould into the shape of a loaf.

Roll out the pastry and cut into a rectangle 30 cm × 60 cm (12" × 24"). Place on an oven tray. Wrap meatloaf in pastry, then seal the edges by brushing with water and pressing firmly together.

Decorate with pastry cut-outs of leaves and roses. Bake at 230°C (450°F) for 10 minutes, then reduce temperature to 220°C (425°F) and bake a further 15–20 minutes or until cooked.

Sausage rolls are pies in disguise

I have always found commercial sausage rolls to be fat-filled, salt-laden apologies for fingerfood. It's true that meat merchants and chefs alike use the worst of their cuts to make sausages and the like. I find it sad, nevertheless a fact. The argument is simple; it's an economic necessity as bovines are not built all of eye fillet.

I believe it would make more sense to discard the fat and the gristle of the lesser cuts, mince the meat, spice it judiciously, protect it with pastry and then charge accordingly.

I've taken many a mauling from European mates who insist that much of the flavour comes from fat and therefore it is an essential ingredient. My argument is to replace the flavour loss of fat with even better flavours. Spices and herbs mixed with crushed nuts or olives would supply vegetable and fruit fats which are poly- or mono-unsaturated and therefore good for us, rather than the animal fats which are presently used.

BEEF PIES

Sausage rolls with tomato or avocado sauce

Makes 30

Ingredients

750 g (1½ lb) lean steak which butcher has minced or finely chopped into mince

1 onion, finely chopped

¼ teaspoon mixed herbs

salt

freshly ground black pepper

1 cup fresh breadcrumbs

3 sheets ready-made puff pastry or 1 quantity puff pastry (see page 10)

1 egg yolk mixed with 2 teaspoons water, for glazing

Method

Place sausage meat, onion, herbs, salt, pepper and breadcrumbs in a bowl and mix well.

Divide the made pastry into two and roll out each into a square. The pastry should be about 3 mm (⅛") thick.

Spoon the sausage mixture in a line down one edge of the pastry. The line of mixture should be about 3 cm (1") high.

Turn the edge of the pastry over the filling, turn again, so that the filling is completely enclosed in the pastry.

Cut any leftover pastry off with a sharp knife. Repeat with the remaining filling and pastry.

Brush the rolls with combined egg yolk and water. Cut into 5 cm (2") pieces.

Place on a baking tray and bake at 220°C (425°F) for 10 minutes. Reduce heat to 190°C (375°F) and bake a further 15 minutes or until the sausage rolls are puffed and golden brown.

BEEF PIES

Tomato sauce

Ingredients

- 1 tablespoon olive oil
- 1 carrot, chopped
- 1 white onion, chopped
- 1 stick celery, chopped
- 1 small cooked beetroot, finely chopped
- 1 tablespoon plain flour
- 1¼ cups chicken stock
- 500 g (1 lb) ripe tomatoes, peeled and chopped
- 1 tablespoon tomato paste
- 1 bouquet garni*
- 1 bay leaf
- freshly ground black pepper
- 1 tablespoon lemon juice

* Collect a few sprigs of fresh herbs from your garden (parsley, thyme, oregano). Tie them together with cotton thread.

Method

Heat the oil in a medium-sized saucepan and add the carrot, onion, celery and beetroot. Cook for a few minutes.

Take the pan off the heat and stir in the flour, then the chicken stock and tomatoes. Peel the tomatoes by holding them on a fork over a flame or dropping them into very hot water for a few minutes until the skin splits and will peel off easily. Add tomato paste, bouquet garni, bay leaf and the pepper.

Bring to the boil, stirring all the time, then simmer for 30 minutes.

Take out the bouquet garni and the bay leaf. Pour the vegetables and stock mixture into your blender and purée it.

Pour it back into the pan, stir in the lemon juice and reheat. If the sauce isn't thick enough, boil it for a few minutes without a lid; it will reduce and thicken.

Heat your sausage roll. Serve it on a crisp lettuce leaf and spoon some tomato sauce over it. Decorate it with a sprig of fresh oregano. You can keep the rest of the sauce in an airtight jar in your fridge for a week.

BEEF PIES

Avocado sauce

Ingredients

2 ripe avocados

⅓ cup chicken stock

1 tablespoon lemon juice

¼ cup cream

3 drops Tabasco Sauce

freshly ground black pepper

Method

Cut the avocados in half. Remove the pip and peel the fruit.

Chop them coarsely and put them in a blender.

Pour in the chicken stock and lemon juice. Purée until smooth.

Pour the purée into a large jug or bowl and stir in the cream, Tabasco Sauce and pepper.

Heat your sausage roll. Serve it on a crisp lettuce leaf and spoon some avocado sauce over it. Decorate it with half a strawberry.

An Aussie in Paris

In principle, pies are perfect. In reality, many are, but there are the odd one or two which leave a lot to be desired. One of those undesirables was baked by myself for a friend who had travelled to Paris to paint.

My mate, Bob Haberfield, had abandoned Melbourne to take on the world with his brushes and palette. For quite a few years we had shared a studio producing fine art to impress ourselves, and commercial art to pay the bills. On those days which were too wet and cold to run to the pub, Bob would open a bottle of red and I'd bake a pie.

'Strewth, mate,' his letters lamented. 'Things are tough in the land of the frog. Those with a fist full of francs get on famously but, if you're a poor, struggling artist ensconced in a garret on the Left Bank ... if you could spare one of your pies and a can of Foster's for m' birthday I'd be greatly indebted.'

Now I'd like you to understand that my mate, Bob, had been a practical joker all his life. This story is not the place to detail the many and various practical jokes he had in his big bag of tricks. Mind you, they weren't malicious and I should assure you mine wasn't intended to be either.

I had the kids collect half a dozen perfectly shaped cow pats which I then baked into pies, spiced with gum leaves. Packed in a box with Foster's and Vegemite, I parcelled the present off to Paris.

An Aussie in Paris

Bob was duly delighted and so invited a gaggle of artist mates to share his good fortune.

'Yeah. M'mate in Melbourne has got a reputation as a bit of a cook and I can tell ya he makes bloody good pies.'

Ceremoniously the pastry-sealed savouries were slid into the jaws of the oven and Foster's served to the expectant tonsils as patterns were drawn with Vegemite on biscuits. I won't elaborate the happenings when the pies were produced and divided, other than to record that it was a débâcle.

Naturally I never ate anything Bob offered me once we were mates again. But I did persuade him to eat a piece of peace-offering pie I packaged and posted to him to replace the cow of a job I'd done for his birthday.

BEEF PIES

Peace-offering pie a. k. a. steak & kidney pie

Serves 6–8

Ingredients

375 g (12 oz) lamb kidneys

2 tablespoons olive oil

½ onion, chopped

750 g (1½ lb) lean steak

1 bay leaf

a good pinch dried thyme

a good pinch ground cloves

freshly ground black pepper

1½ cups beef stock

1 cup beer

375 g (12 oz) shortcrust pastry (1½ quantity of shortcrust pastry, see page 8)

1 egg, beaten

Method

Skin the kidneys, slice them thinly and sauté them gently for a couple of minutes in the oil in a large heavy frying pan, moving them around all the time. Toss in the onion, sauté another couple of minutes, then take the pan off the heat.

Oil a pie dish or pudding basin. Cut the steak into 1 cm × 5 cm (½" × 2") strips and put it into the dish. Sprinkle with the crumbled bay leaf, thyme, cloves and freshly ground black pepper.

Pour in the stock and beer and pop the dish, covered, into the oven at 180°C (350°F) for 45 minutes.

Take it out of the oven, stir in the kidneys and onions, and cover with a 3 mm (⅛") layer of shortcrust pastry. Brush with beaten egg, then put the pie back in the oven and cook for another 20–25 minutes until the pastry is golden.

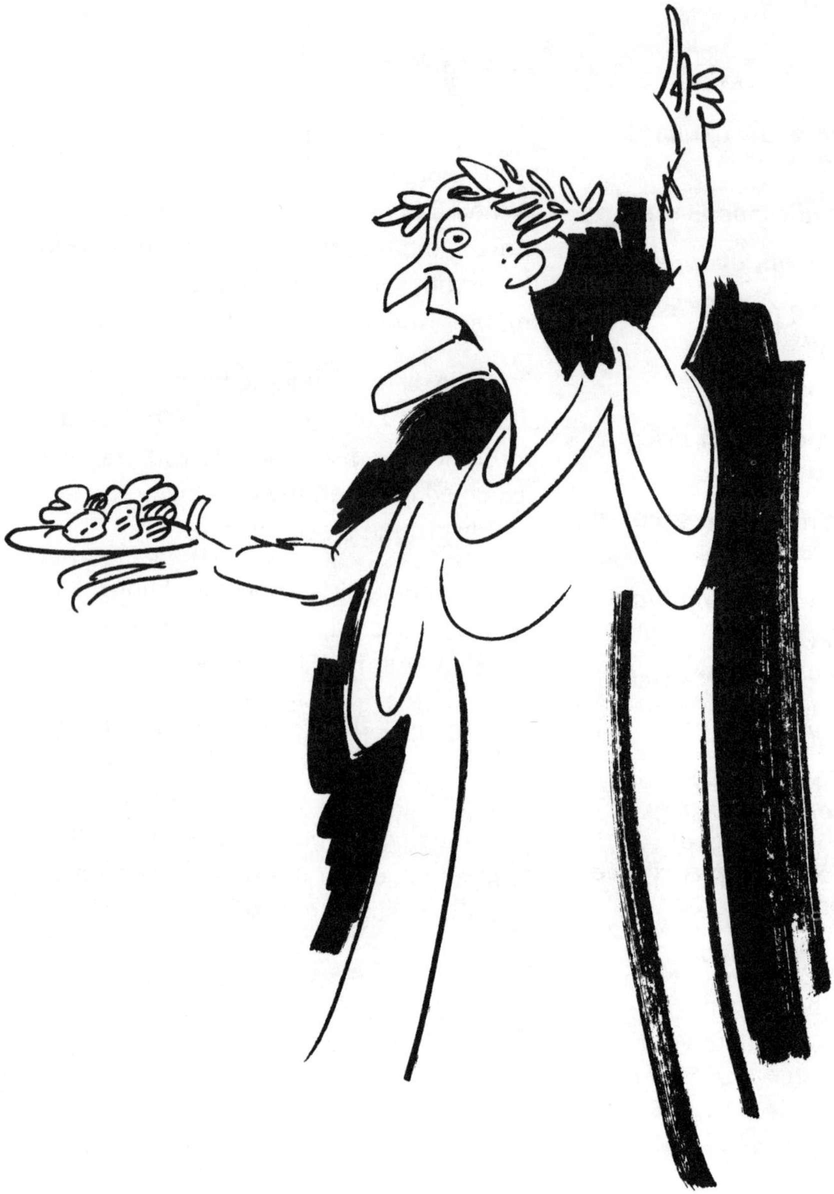

A corned beef and cabbage story

The debauched, gluttonous, criminally insane Roman Emperor, Claudius, demanded that the Senate vote on whether corned beef and cabbage was the most marvellous of foods. The Senate dutifully voted that, indeed, it was.

Cabbage at that time was a most expensive vegetable even though, before the Romans dominated the world, the Greeks had used it as gut-filler. The Greek philosopher, Socrates, told his student, Plato, if he ate lots of cabbage he would not have to kowtow to his betters. The student replied if he kowtowed to his betters he would not have to eat cabbage. As for corned beef, it was simply what we call silverside, pumped with salt to preserve it because refrigeration was unknown and ice extremely expensive and not always readily available.

The Romans wrapped much of their food in pastry. Not only for the added flavour and texture, but also to make it easily transportable.

My research does not reveal whether the mad Claudius and his cronies ever contemplated a corned beef and cabbage pie but, if they didn't, they should have. With the outside fat cut off, corned beef is as lean as the Tower of Pisa, and cabbage, of course, is full of fibre and other good things which make us tickety-boo.

BEEF PIES

Corned beef pie No. 1

To cook the corned beef you'll need:

Ingredients

1 × 2 kg (4 lb) piece silverside

1 cup fresh water

1 teaspoon dried oregano

freshly ground black pepper

1 carrot, peeled and sliced

1 white onion stuck with 3 whole cloves

¼ cup chopped celery leaves

1 bay leaf

Method

Put the silverside in a pressure cooker (see opposite if you don't have one).

Cover it with water and bring it to the boil without the lid on, or at least not under pressure.

Immediately drain off the water because that gets rid of all the excess salt.

Now put the meat back into the pressure cooker, add one cup of fresh water, the oregano, freshly ground black pepper (but don't put any salt on it because it's salty stuff), the carrot, onion, celery tops and bay leaf.

Put on the lid and pop on the weight and place it over a high heat. When the weight begins to jiggle, turn the heat down low and cook for about 45 minutes.

BEEF PIES

No pressure cooker?

You use the same ingredients except you'll need more than one cup of fresh water. First, just boil up the meat in a saucepan, then get rid of the salty water. Put the meat back in the saucepan with all the other ingredients. Cover with fresh water, pop on a lid and bring to the boil. Lower the heat and simmer for 30 minutes. Then remove it from the stove and wrap it all up (saucepan, lid and all) in a blanket and leave overnight. By morning it'll be beautifully cooked without shrinking.

Now the cabbage

Ingredients for an individual pie

- *handful of cabbage, shredded*
- *½ brown onion, sliced*
- *4 black olives*
- *2 garlic cloves*
- *splash of white wine*
- *salt*
- *freshly ground black pepper*
- *1 thick slice of cooked silverside*
- *1 sheet puff pastry*
- *1 egg, beaten*
- *poppyseeds*

Method

Put the cabbage in a pan with the brown onion, pitted black olives and the juice of the two cloves of garlic.

Splash in a little white wine and soften the cabbage. Sprinkle with a little salt and some freshly ground pepper. Cook for no more than a minute.

Cut a slice of silverside as thick as your thumbnail is wide. Dice it into bite-sized pieces and stir it into the cabbage mixture which you have taken off the heat.

Place your corned beef and cabbage into a pie dish that is large enough to accommodate it. Cover it with puff pastry. Brush the top with a beaten egg, sprinkle it with poppyseeds and place it in a hot oven 230°C (450°F) for 20 minutes or until it is golden brown.

BEEF PIES

Corned beef pie No. 2 Serves 4

Ingredients

1 tablespoon olive oil

1 white onion, finely chopped

1 clove garlic, crushed

250 g (8 oz) cooked corned beef, diced finely

2 tablespoons tomato purée

good pinch dried oregano

freshly ground black pepper

2 tomatoes, thickly sliced

375 g (12 oz) boiled potatoes

2 tablespoons butter

milk, if needed

2 spring onions, chopped

Method

Heat the oil in a saucepan, throw in the onion and garlic and cook until transparent.

Toss in the corned beef, then add the tomato purée. Sprinkle with oregano and freshly ground black pepper. Stir and heat, but don't cook.

Put this mixture in the base of a pie dish and cover with a layer of sliced tomato.

Mash the potatoes with the butter whilst they're still hot, adding a little milk if needed. They should be light and creamy, but not sloppy.

Stir in the spring onions, then pile the mixture on top of the meat. Don't smooth over the potatoes; a rough surface is desirable.

Dot with more butter and sprinkle with freshly ground black pepper and a little more oregano. Pop it in the oven at 200°C (400° F) until the top is brown and crunchy, then serve.

Budget pie

Economists cut their budgetary pie into accurate assessments of how the finances are flowing. An 8.3 per cent of something or other is sliced next to 17.2 per cent of another equally important part of their shenanigans, and so on and so on, until the pie is apportioned to allow even a dullard to understand the main issues quickly and easily.

Why didn't these mathematicians choose the wheel, or a round of cheese, or Mademoiselle's beret for that matter? I suggest they chose the pie because everyone is familiar with it; it's non-threatening; it's historical and folksy; and it's got a great taste into the bargain.

So let's look at making a pie large enough for us to cut into portions to suit the size of the appetite of your family or friends. Little Johnnie or Jill is well satisfied with a finger width of pie, but huge Uncle Harry, the demolisher, needs a hefty hunk, Aunt Maude a gentle slice and Mum not as much as Dad.

Now, since economics have inspired our Budget Pie, it's appropriate also, I think, for us to concern ourselves with economy. So a Budget Pie recipe it is.

BEEF PIES

Budget pie No. 1 Serves 4–6

Now, one of the cheaper cuts of meat is gravy beef.

How to cook gravy beef

Chop the gravy beef into a few large chunks and brown it on the stove top.

Cover with 1½ cups of water and simmer gently with the lid on for 1½ hours. Add more water if necessary.

Ingredients

- 500 g (1 lb) gravy beef
- 1 medium carrot, cooked and diced
- ¾ cup cooked lima beans
- ¾ cup cooked peas
- freshly ground black pepper
- salt
- 3–4 sheets puff pastry
- 1 egg, beaten

Method

Dice the cooked gravy beef finely, mix with the carrots, lima beans and green peas. Sprinkle with salt and pepper.

Place this mixture in a pie dish, top it with puff pastry, brush it with beaten egg and pop it into a hot oven at 230°C (450°F) for 15–20 minutes.

Serving suggestions

This recipe works equally well for small pies as it does for larger pies. If you made a large pie, lift off the cooked pastry lid and cut it into segments, and put them aside. Spoon out the pie mixture onto individual plates and spoon the gravy over it. Pop on a piece of pastry as a cap to the pie's contents, place a salad beside it and serve.

BEEF PIES

Budget pie No. 2 Serves 4–6

If you have discarded the gravy beef from Budget Pie No. 1 because its quality was not what you desired on the day, you can still use its juices to add flavour to this pie.

Ingredients

¾ cup (approximately) reserved gravy beef stock

1 Spanish onion, sliced and diced

1 cm (½") fresh ginger, finely grated

500 g (1 lb) uncooked meat, chopped into bite-sized pieces

2–2½ cups spinach leaves

3 cups cooked, mashed sweet potato

3 sheets filo pastry

¾ cup grated tasty cheese

1 egg, beaten

sprinkle of mustard seeds

Method

Spoon the liquid which remains in the gravy beef saucepan into a pie dish whilst it's still hot. Throw in the Spanish onion and ginger, and allow it to go cold. It is important to cool the liquid because when you tip in the chopped meat of your choice, you don't want it to overcook, which will happen if it's put into a piping hot sauce and then placed in a hot oven.

Chunk cut the raw spinach leaves. Cover the pie mixture with a layer of spinach the thickness of your little finger. Cover the spinach leaves with the same thickness of sweet potato. Top with three layers of filo pastry interlaced with grated tasty cheese.

Brush the pastry with beaten egg and sprinkle mustard seeds on it, pushing them into the pastry so they don't pop all over the inside of the oven once they're heated. This very special pie goes into a hot oven (230°C/450°F) for about 20 minutes or until the pastry is golden brown.

BEEF PIES

Shepherd's pie Serves 8–10

Ingredients

1 tablespoon olive oil

1 kg (2 lb) minced steak

2 white onions, finely chopped

2 carrots, finely chopped

1 tablespoon tomato paste

good pinch of dried oregano

¼ cup beef stock

1 cup cooked mixed vegetables (anything cluttering your fridge!)

5 medium-sized potatoes, boiled and mashed

1 tablespoon butter

Method

Heat the olive oil in a large saucepan; drop in the steak and brown it.

Pour off any excess fat that comes from the meat, then stir in the onions and carrots, and cook for about 5 minutes.

Stir in the tomato paste and oregano, pour in the stock and add the other vegetables.

Pour it all into an ovenproof casserole, top with mashed potatoes and dot with butter.

Sprinkle a few more dried oregano leaves on top and pop it into the oven to bake at 180°C (350°F) for 30 minutes until the potatoes are a golden brown.

Lamb, pork, veal and rabbit pies

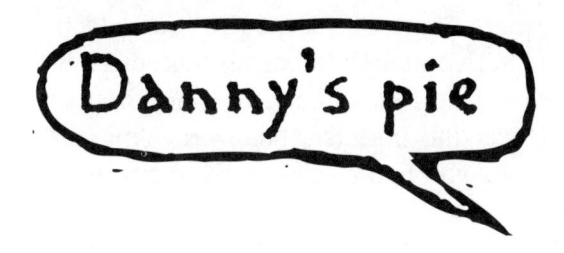

Danny's pie

'May the good lord forgive your ignorance. Pies are as Irish as Paddy's pigs,' choked Danny. 'The Poms have been stealing everything which is good and proper from God's own green land since Himself deserted them for being pagan and painting their nakedness in blue woad.'

I let that go through to the keeper and swung the conversation around to a less explosive subject. How many were actually attending Danny's birthday party and would they all be sharing the pie I was preparing?

'God bless ya. Of course, everyone will come and all will rejoice that the Almighty has seen fit to let me keep breathing His sweet air,' Danny chortled before downing a pot of half rum, half beer.

'The rum's to keep the cold out and the beer's there to make it go further,' Danny explained, splashing the two liquids together as he, yet again, filled his pot. His two brothers were keeping pace with him to ensure that no disagreements would fester over one of the siblings getting more than another.

It was certainly true that they were more attentive to the mixing of the brew than the mixing of the ingredients for a pie or two which I would bake to help celebrate the occasion of the old Irishman's birthday.

The Glynn brothers lived in an area known as Micalong which was in the Brindabella Mountains between Canberra and Tumut. Danny confessed that, although he considered himself to be a chef worthy of the cause, it was not right and proper for him to perform such a menial task on the occasion of his birthday.

'So you'll do it for me then, won't you?' he directed. 'Use what-

Danny's pie

ever you want, except go easy on the Cocky's Joy and I'm a bit short of powdered milk.'

For those unenlightened readers, Cocky's Joy is golden syrup which, as you can well imagine I hadn't contemplated as an ingredient in my about-to-be-baked pie. Nor had I considered the inclusion of powdered milk. But Danny was off, enthusiastically regaling his brothers and a gaggle of guests who had already arrived and who were well into the grog.

A Shepherd's Pie seemed appropriate as the boys kept a few sheep amongst the blackberries and saplings on their run. The meat was fresher than Doris Day's complexion and therefore had to be very finely diced to hide its toughness. There was some pork which required the same treatment and into which I chopped some bacon. I topped and tailed some French beans and added broad beans to them and the kernels from fresh corn. You see, the boys had their own vegetable garden, which made my lot a lot easier.

I mixed the vegetables with the meat and splashed the lot with Worcestershire Sauce and, despite their howls of protest, a goodly splash of the rum and beer mixture. I sprinkled on some salt and pepper and mashed the potatoes which I smoothed with butter which had been freshly churned before the grog had been opened.

Now, for pie dishes we had an assortment of various tin, cast iron and enamelled odds and sods. It was into these that the pie mixture was spooned, then topped with the creamy potatoes. I finely chopped onion and pushed it into the topping, then put the whole lot into the jaws of a giant oven which Danny and his brothers had rescued from a defunct bush hospital.

It was a heavy, cast iron affair, fuelled by wood twenty-four hours a day. Twenty-five minutes or so later, the pies were on the table. They were all shapes and sizes which somehow made the gathering more festive.

But, by now, the numbers had increased as had their alcohol levels. The pies were devoured in a twinkling and more were demanded. Piano accordions, mouth organs and fiddles appeared, and the party was in full swing.

A little later — around one in the morning — someone noticed

Danny's pie

that Danny was not about and hadn't been seen for half an hour or more.

'He's fallen over outside and snapped one of his frail little legs,' cried his brother.

'Begorrah, his bones are as brittle as dried twigs in a drought,' chorused the other brother.

And so the party swept through windows and doors to scour the surrounding bush for the birthday boy.

'Danny! Danny!' they cried. But to no avail.

'The pigs have got the poor old bugger!' someone shouted.

'Well then, he's done for. For their tusks are razor sharp and they're tough, hard little buggers.'

'And so was Danny,' someone wailed. 'He would have put up a good fight, you can bet all that's good.'

The party sadly retired inside and toasted and toasted and toasted the missing, presumed dead, Danny.

'He was the best brother a boy could ever have.' 'God loved him as His own.' 'He was kind to all animals and his neighbours alike,' The comments were flung in the air as grog was flung down throats.

An hour later, Danny burst into the room as sprightly as a fife player on St Patrick's Day.

'Well, boyos. Where's m' drop o' the doings?'

Jaws dropped in unison.

'God be praised! You're alive! Where've ya been, Danny?'

'I needed a little rest, so I pillowed m' head in m' arms after I'd crawled down a wombat hole to keep warm.'

'And no doubt you took a bottle with ya, ya secretive old bastard,' cried the brothers, giving him a good whack under the ear.

'Ya frightened the b'jeezus out of the lot of us. Not one man wasn't worried sick over ya,' said another, giving him a foot up the bum.

'Ya need to be taught a bloody good lesson,' they chorused, all hopping in, punching and kicking the old bloke until he went down.

'That'll teach ya to have us worried sick over ya. It'll take me a week to recover from the shock!' they shouted. 'It's a disgraceful

Danny's pie

thing ya've done to us. We were going to build a memorial cairn outside in the backyard to commemorate our love for ya,' they said, giving him a final kick before going back to the grog.

The third lot of pies was forgotten in the oven as I attended the old man's injuries. A broken wrist, a couple of broken ribs and a lot of bruises kept him quiet for the rest of the week.

The pies had burned to a crisp, the party forgotten, but the events of his birthday will live on in our minds forever.

LAMB, PORK, VEAL AND RABBIT PIES

Lamb pie and forcemeat balls Serves 10–12

Ingredients

1½ quantity puff pastry (see page 10)

750 g (1½ lb) uncooked lean lamb, cut into small cubes

½ cup seedless raisins, sliced in half

½ cup sultanas

¼ teaspoon ground cloves

¼ teaspoon ground nutmeg

¼ teaspoon ground mace

salt and pepper

sprinkle of sugar

250 g (8 oz) white grapes, blanched for one minute in boiling water

500 g (1 lb) new potatoes, sliced

1 tablespoon candied lemon and orange peel

Method

Line a large, deep, buttered pie dish with pastry and cover with a layer of lamb cubes, then a layer of raisins and sultanas. Use about half the quantities of lamb, raisins and sultanas.

Sprinkle with some of the cloves, nutmeg, mace, salt and pepper.

Then add a layer of forcemeat balls (see next page), more cloves, nutmeg, mace, a little sugar and a layer of grapes.

Top with a layer of sliced potatoes and a few pieces of candied lemon and orange peel.

Add another layer of lamb and repeat the other layers.

Dot with butter, and cover with pastry. Bake in the oven at 180°C (350°F) for 1¼ hours. If pastry becomes too brown, cover with foil and continue cooking.

When the pie is cooked, lift off the lid and put it on a separate plate. Cut it into wedges from the centre out.

Pour the hot wine and egg sauce (see next page) into the pie and stir well.

Place the pieces of pie lid around the edges of the pie, sticking into the inside edge. Serve very hot. →

49

LAMB, PORK, VEAL AND RABBIT PIES

Forcemeat balls

Ingredients

250 g (8 oz) finely minced lamb

250 g (8 oz) finely minced pork

2 tablespoons onions, finely chopped

¼ teaspoon marjoram

¼ teaspoon ground mace

salt and pepper

1 egg

Method

Mix all the ingredients together and make into 4 cm (1½") balls.

Hot wine and egg sauce

Ingredients

600 ml (20 fl oz) red wine

4 egg yolks

2 tablespoons lemon juice

salt and pepper

Method

Heat the wine and when it is almost boiling, pour it over the egg yolks.

Stir in the lemon juice and season to taste.

LAMB, PORK, VEAL AND RABBIT PIES

Large meat pie with filo pastry Serves 4–6

Ingredients

1 medium onion, finely chopped

2 tablespoons olive oil

500 g (1 lb) lean lamb or beef, minced

2 tablespoons pine nuts

salt

freshly ground black pepper

½ teaspoon ground allspice

5 tablespoons water

extra olive oil

8–10 sheets filo pastry

Method

Fry the onion in the olive oil until soft and golden. Add the meat and fry lightly until it changes colour.

Stir in the pine nuts and fry for a further 2 minutes. Stir in salt, pepper and allspice. Moisten with 5 tablespoons water. Cook for a few more minutes until the water is absorbed.

Oil a large square ovenproof dish. Fit four or five sheets of pastry in it, one on top of the other, brushing each sheet with oil and folding them up so that they overlap the sides of the dish.

Spread the meat mixture over this and cover with the remaining sheets of pastry, brushing oil between each layer as well as on top.

Bake the pie in the oven at 160°C (325°F) for about 45 minutes. Increase the heat to 220°C (425°F) for another 5–10 minutes or until the top of the pie is crisp and golden.

LAMB, PORK, VEAL AND RABBIT PIES

Chinese meat pie Serves 4–6

This meat pie should not be made in advance because its flavour would dissipate and its texture would harden.

Ingredients

500 g (1 lb) ground lean pork

2 tablespoons light soy sauce

1 tablespoon dry sherry

¼ teaspoon salt

¼ teaspoon sugar

sprinkling black pepper

1 tablespoon cornflour, dissolved in ¼ cup chicken stock with 1 tablespoon sesame oil

½ cup finely minced ribs of iceberg lettuce

⅛ teaspoon salt

Method

Chop the ground meat on a chopping board using close strokes across the mound, flipping it, and chopping across the other side. Do this four or five times until the meat is very smooth.

Put it in a large bowl, add the soy sauce, sherry, ¼ teaspoon salt, sugar, and black pepper. Mix well.

Add the dissolved cornflour and stir in a circular motion until it is evenly blended. The meat, when pinched between your fingers, should feel soft and wet. If dry and cakey, add a little more stock and stir some more.

Cut the thick bottom parts and ribs of the lettuce into fine shreds. Hold them in a bundle and mince, to make ½ cup. They offer no flavour but release juices to moisturise the meat during cooking. Toss them lightly with ⅛ teaspoon salt, add to the meat and mix.

Place the meat mixture in a soup or pie plate and smooth it into a mound with a wet knife. Steam over medium-high heat for 30 minutes in a covered steamer. Remove the plate to a serving platter and serve.

Raised pork pie Serves 4

Pork pies are eaten cold so they are perfect for picnics or as a gourmet snack. They are made with hot-water crust pastry.

Jelly

Ingredients

bones from pork, plus veal knuckle or two pig's trotters

1 large carrot, sliced

1 medium onion stuck with 2 cloves

bouquet garni

12 peppercorns

Method

Make the jelly first. Cut the meat and fat off a pork bone and/or spareribs. Set aside the meat and fat for the filling. Put all ingredients into a large saucepan and fill with water to within 2.5 cm (1") of the top. Simmer for 3–5 hours. Do not add salt.

Strain off the stock into a clean pan and boil it down to about 450 ml (15 fl oz).

Add salt and more pepper to taste and leave to cool. This jelly can be made a day in advance of the pie. →

LAMB, PORK, VEAL AND RABBIT PIES

Filling

Ingredients

1 kg (2 lb) pork shoulder or spareribs, with 1 part fat to 2 parts lean meat

250 g (8 oz) very thinly cut bacon rashers

1 teaspoon fresh sage, chopped

½ teaspoon each of: nutmeg, cinnamon, ground cloves, allspice

salt

freshly ground black pepper

1 teaspoon anchovy sauce

1½ quantity hot-water crust pastry (see page 12)

1 egg, beaten

Method

Next make the filling. Chop the pork, or mince it coarsely. Then mince half of it finely with two rashers of the bacon.

Mix all the pork together, add the sage and spices, salt and pepper, and the anchovy sauce.

Fry a small piece of this mixture to test the flavour, remembering that dishes to be eaten cold always need a stronger seasoning than dishes to be eaten hot.

Make the hot-water crust pastry and mould the case (see page 12), taking care to leave no cracks through which the pie juices will be able to escape. If the pastry slides down the mould, it's still a little hot; leave it for a while then start again. Remember to set aside some pastry for the lid.

Lay the remaining rashers of bacon over the bottom and lower sides to form an inner lining.

Pack in the filling and mound it up nicely at the top to support the lid.

Moisten the pastry rim with water and lay on the reserved pastry which has been rolled out as a lid.

Trim and knock up the edges, make a hole in the centre and decorate with pastry leaves and roses.

LAMB, PORK, VEAL AND RABBIT PIES

Cut a strip of stiff paper to roll up and push into the hole; this keeps it open during cooking. Brush with beaten egg.

Bake in the oven at 200°C (400°F) for 30 minutes then lower the temperature to 160°C (325°F) and cook for another 1½–2 hours. Let the pie cool a little, then remove the mould, brush the sides with beaten egg and return the pie to the oven to brown. Protect the lid with foil.

Remove the roll of paper from the hole and, if the jelly has set firm, melt it till it is runny but cool, then pour it into the hot pie a little at a time, through the centre hole, using a kitchen funnel. Leave pie overnight before eating.

LAMB, PORK, VEAL AND RABBIT PIES

Loin of pork cooked in pastry Serves 8–10

Ingredients

1 × 1.5 kg (3 lb) boned loin of pork

1 carrot

1 onion

6 cloves

bunch of fresh herbs

salt

6 peppercorns

½ quantity puff pastry (see page 10)

Method

Cook the loin of pork in water with the carrot, onion, cloves, herbs, salt and peppercorns for about 40 minutes.

Let it cool in the stock.

Roll out the puff pastry. Place the well-drained loin of pork on the pastry, bringing the sides of the pastry to meet on top and join together.

Place, upside down, on a baking tray and decorate with any leftover pastry.

Bake in the oven at 180°C (350°F) until browned. Let it go cold, then slice and serve.

Bacon, spinach and tomato pasta pie Serves 6

Ingredients

olive oil

3 rashers lean bacon, roughly chopped

1 small onion, finely chopped

1 clove garlic, crushed

1 small red capsicum, cut into thin strips

3 tomatoes, finely chopped

1 cup spinach, washed and chopped

2 tablespoons tomato paste

¼ cup grated Parmesan cheese

375 g (12 oz) pasta, cooked and drained

Method

Heat a little olive oil in a saucepan and cook bacon, onion, garlic and capsicum until onion is soft.

Add tomato, spinach and tomato paste and cook for 3 minutes or until vegetables are heated through. Do not overcook.

Heat spinach sauce and pasta together, then place it onto a double thickness rectangle of baking paper. Sprinkle with Parmesan cheese. Bring paper together to cover pasta, twist ends closed.

Bake in oven at 180°C (350°F) for 8 minutes. Remove the paper (of course!) and serve with salad and crusty bread.

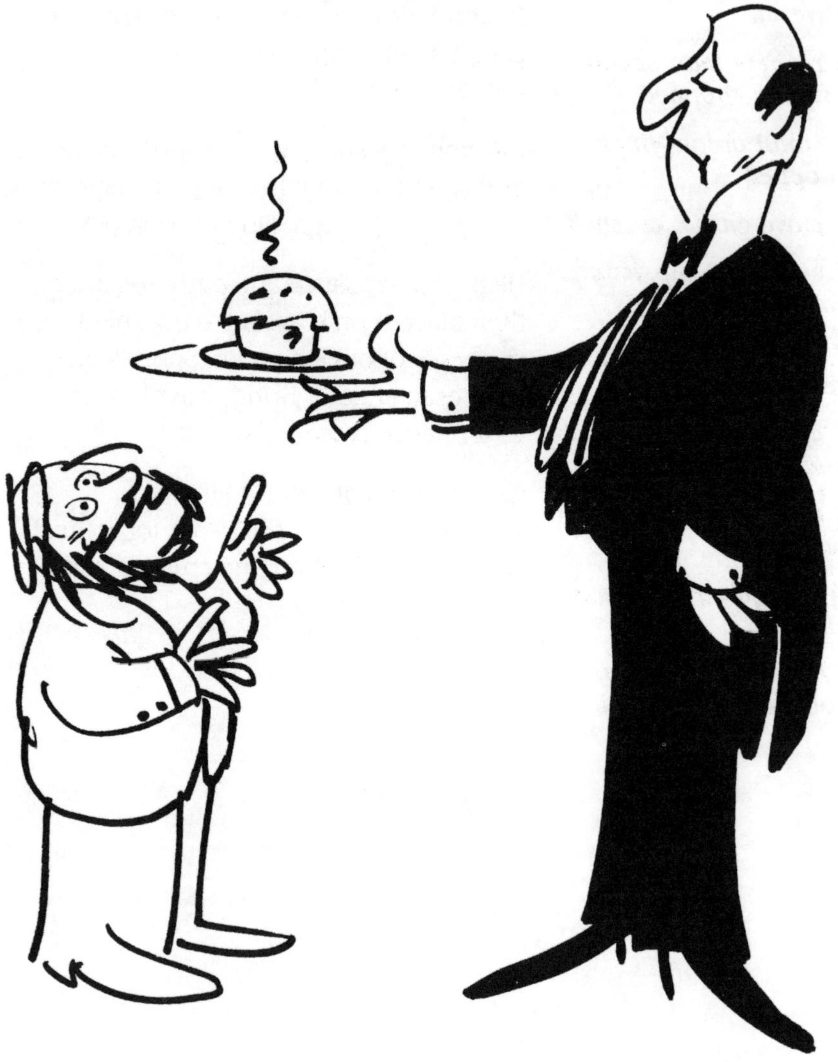

Pompous pie

The Pommies claim the pie as their own although it's hard to think of a single nation which doesn't glorify pastry-wrapped food. Certainly the English are famous for their water pastry pies, cottage pies, Shepherd's Pies along with other pies of every type, colour and dimension. They eat them hot or cold, on plates with vegetables or clutched in gloved hands at the soccer. Partridge pies for breakfast, turbot pies for lunch or beef, kidney and bacon pies with warmed claret to finish the day.

I was served a pie by a gentleman's gentleman whilst waiting for the great gentleman himself to present himself to both me and the day. The morning was crisp but sunny and the grandfather clock chimed half past ten.

'His lordship finishes *The Times* and his morning tiffin before talking to anyone, other than the Prime Minister, or those members of the Royal Family with whom he is familiar. Nevertheless he would scold me if I didn't make you comfortable while you collected yourself for meeting with his lordship.'

Not many minutes later, the butler re-emerged to usher in a serving wench adroitly manipulating a silver tray adorned with an antique tea service and a salver, covered with a decorated silver dome, which hid a meat pie of magnificence.

Half the pie was served to me with a napkin and a spoon. No sauce was offered as the minced veal flesh flavour was far too delicate to be interrupted by the intrusion of any other taste. The pastry was flaky, the meat moist with its own juices and those of the small gooseberries which marbled the meat. The full pie was the size of a saucer, therefore my half was elegant sufficiency for morning tea.

Pompous pie

His lordship arrived, bedecked in grey flannel trousers, a Paisley dressing gown with cuffs and collar of a superior felt, the whole ensemble tied together with a cardinal-red sash which was matched with a cravat. M' lord looked like an aged Errol Flynn with buck teeth which I think was the cause of his lisp.

After we'd discussed the reason for my visit and I was about to leave, I boldly asked, if it was not a family secret, could he oblige me with the recipe for the pie.

He stared at me incredulously.

'Good God, man,' he oathed. 'James buys them from the local store. A chap can't afford a jolly cook now the bloody Government takes every penny that pater left me. To say nothing of the amount they carve off the pittance I earn from having the local peasants flog their grubby boots through my palace.'

Once I arrived home, I reproduced the peer's morning tea and called it Pompous Pie. If gooseberries are unobtainable, replace them with seedless grapes.

P.S. Deleting the heading 'Pompous Pie', I sent the recipe to his lordship only to receive the reply that it was nothing like the one he served, therefore he will instruct the bakery from now on to follow my recipe and serve them as Peter's Pies.

Pompous pie

Ingredients for an individual pie

1 sheet ready-made shortcrust pastry

125 g (4 oz) fillet of veal, shaved

garlic salt and white pepper

2 dessertspoons of sauterne or fruity chardonnay

8 or so plump gooseberries or green grapes

2 tablespoons of fresh mung beans (Living Green brand are the best)

pinch of dried thyme

1 medium-sized, cooked, mashed potato

1 onion, diced

1 sheet ready-made puff pastry

Method

Blind bake the pastry in an ovenproof pie dish.

Sprinkle the veal lightly with garlic salt and dust with white pepper. Create a mound the size of an apple and pour the sauterne or fruity chardonnay over it. Mix in the gooseberries (or grapes) and the mung beans.

Work the mixture with your fingers until the meat has taken up the liquid.

Dust the inside of the pastry base lightly with the thyme. Pop in the veal mixture and top it with mashed potato mixed with the raw onion. The depth of the potato should be no greater than the thickness of your little finger.

Pop on a bonnet of puff pastry. Cook the pie in a hot oven at 220°C (425°F) for 20–25 minutes until the pastry is golden brown.

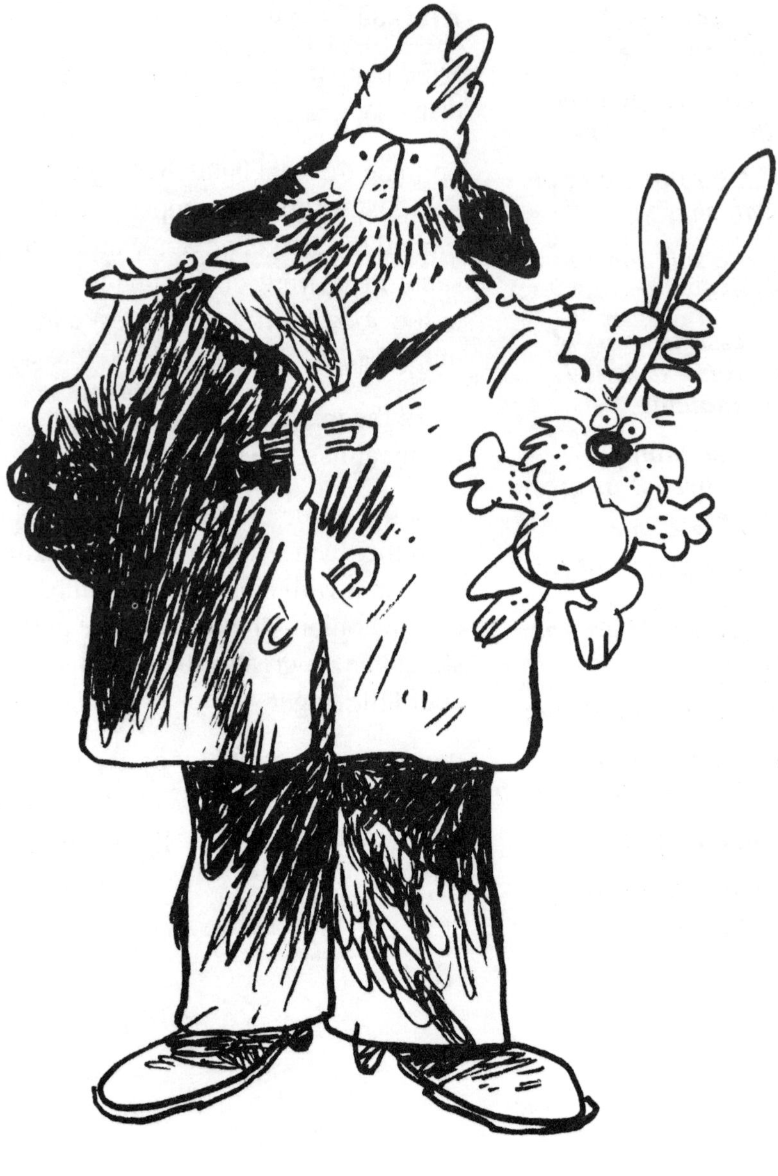

Rabbit pie Serves 4

Ingredients

250 g (8 oz) streaky bacon, chopped

½ teaspoon ground mace

1 level teaspoon salt

4 tablespoons finely chopped parsley

4 tablespoons finely chopped chives

1 teaspoon finely chopped basil

the livers of the rabbits (or 6 chicken livers)

2 young rabbits, cut into small joints

⅔ cup red wine

125 g (4 oz) butter

4 extra rashers bacon

½ quantity shortcrust pastry (see page 8) or 2–3 sheets ready-made pastry

Method

Pound half the chopped bacon with the mace, salt, parsley, chives, basil and livers to make a fine paste.

Line the bottom of a pie dish with the paste, then put the pieces of rabbit on top, closely packed.

Pour the wine over the top and make another paste with the remaining half of the chopped bacon and the butter.

Spread on top of the rabbit, cover with the rashers of bacon and top with pastry.

Bake in the oven at 180°C (350°F) for about an hour until the rabbit is cooked and the pastry golden brown. Have a peek after about 40 minutes and cover the pastry with buttered brown paper if it is starting to brown.

Chicken pies

Skinny

We all know now why the chicken crossed the road. It was to get to the other side. I am now about to reveal what its fate was once it was found on the other side of the road. It was popped into a pie. Or so I assert.

You see, I saw it happen when I was a young boy living in the bush.

An adventurous, wily old rooster scratched its way under the netting of a chook pen behind the pub. With great glee and cock-a-doodle-doos it triumphantly led its harem of plump young hens across the very rarely used road, to scratch in the paddocks beside our place.

My mother's boyfriend, a tough timber cutter, happened to be home honing his axes. He was hungry. Quick as a flash he hurdled the fence, grabbed the plumpest of the escapees and set about preparing it for the pot. Then my mother intervened to convince the chicken plucker that a pie would be preferable. And so it came about.

The pie was made and served at the same time as there was an impatient knocking at the back door.

'Police here,' an authoritative voice rattled the window panes.

Skinny, for that was my mother's live-in lover's name and whom I called 'uncle', opened the door.

'Come in, Col,' he said to the copper. 'We're just about to have a feed of rosemary and rabbit pie.'

Glasses of what we called burgundy were poured, and the pie

Skinny

was cut and served, while the member of the local constabulary accused Skinny of nicking the publican's chicken.

'What makes you think that?' laughed Skinny. Skinny was so-called because of his huge shoulders and muscular body developed from cutting down ironbark for telegraph poles.

'There's feathers all over the paddock at your back gate,' frowned the law.

'Must be the cockatoos moulting,' grinned Skinny.

'This tastes remarkably like chicken,' continued Colin the copper.

'It's the way we cook the rabbit,' the axeman assured him. 'Good isn't it?'

Everyone agreed to another glass of wine to accompany the rest of the rabbit.

CHICKEN PIES

Chicken pie Serves 4–6

Ingredients

1 × 2 kg (4 lb) roasting chicken

1 beef marrow bone

500 g (1 lb) carrots, chopped

250 g (8 oz) turnips, chopped

3 sticks celery, chopped

1 onion stuck with 3 whole cloves

1 garlic head, unpeeled

salt

¼ cup brandy

3 tablespoons butter

3 tablespoons flour

4 egg yolks

¼ cup cream

¼ cup cultured sour cream

freshly ground white pepper

½ quantity puff pastry (see page 10) or 2–3 sheets of ready-made puff pastry

Method

Put the chicken and the beef bone into a large saucepan. Add water to cover and bring slowly to the boil. Skim, then add the carrots, turnips, celery, onion and garlic. Bring to the boil again and skim. Sprinkle very lightly with salt. Cover and simmer for 45 minutes or until the chicken is quite tender.

Take the chicken from the saucepan and let it cool. Cut the chicken meat off the bone and then cut it into bite-sized pieces. Discard the skin. Put the chicken meat into a small saucepan with the brandy and let it simmer, covered, over a very low heat for 10 minutes.

Add the chicken bones to the liquid in the large saucepan and boil until you have a strong, flavoursome broth. Strain.

Now make the sauce. Melt the butter in a small saucepan. Take the pan off the heat and stir in the flour to make a roux. Slowly and gradually add two cups of the chicken broth to the roux making sure the mixture remains smooth.

Put the pan back on the heat and let the contents cook for 10 minutes. Blend three of the egg yolks, the cream and sour cream together and, with the pan off the heat, stir them into the sauce. Bring it slowly to a simmer and, stirring →

CHICKEN PIES

constantly, simmer until it's thick and smooth. Add the salt and pepper to your taste.

Put the chicken meat into a 23 cm (9") pie dish and pour the sauce over it. Let it cool.

Roll out the puff pastry into a round, slightly larger than the pie dish, and cover the chicken meat. Press the edges firmly to make a tight seal. Make a couple of holes with the point of a sharp knife and brush with the remaining egg yolk.

Bake in the oven at 190°C (375°F) for about 25 minutes. Serve very hot.

The night father stuck his head in the gas oven

I flew from Melbourne to Sydney for the purpose of spending a few days with my father. I enjoyed his company as we shared many interests — good red wine, cigars, port, Mendelssohn, relating adventures — all of which we combined while we enjoyed a snifter of brandy. Oh, and I forgot one of the most important topics of all: fine food, as he was a fabulous chef.

He was founder of the Escoffier Society which comprised a group of eminent foodies who met once a month to eat and discuss fine fare. When it was my father's turn to cook, he invited me as a guest to the Society. So the reason for my trip was twofold.

The plane flight was uneventful and, after a cab ride to Kirribilli where my father lived in a flat which fronted Rushcutter's Bay, we embraced and father informed me he'd just popped a pie into the oven for our supper.

'Also,' he said, drawing the cork from a bottle of full-bodied burgundy, 'the pie is the same as I will serve at the Society's meeting next Monday. I want your opinion, son,' he said, pouring the dark liquid into clear crystal glasses.

Twenty-five minutes later, pater sprang from his chair to withdraw from the oven his flaky pastry pie which he would then dissect into portions.

The night father stuck his head in the gas oven

A strident shriek of horror flung from the kitchen.

'The bloody pie's still white! What the hell's happened?'

'You forgot to turn on the gas, old man,' I suggested with a grin.

'The knob's on,' he snarled, jabbing at it with his finger, 'but there's no bloody gas.'

I declined to stick my head in the oven for all the obvious reasons but my father had no such concerns.

'Maybe the outlets are blocked,' he cried dropping to his knees and thrusting his bearded face into the dark interior.

You're right, dear reader.

'I can't see a thing,' came his muffled voice, 'Give us a match.'

'Don't be bloody silly,' I said.

'I'm telling you there's no gas,' he snapped.

The night father stuck his head in the gas oven

Reluctantly I handed him his cigar lighter which he flicked into flame. There were several mumbles, then a cry of frightened rage as my father yanked his head out of the oven, his beard and what was left of his hair, smouldering.

I stupidly laughed which sent him into a tower of rage as he shoved his head under the kitchen sink tap.

What had happened was simply this. The gas company had cut off supply as they mended a main in the street. My father had forgotten the notice he'd been sent which told him the times the gas would be turned off and when it would be turned on again. And that, of course, is what caused the hissing of gas into the oven, which instantly ignited due to the presence of the cigar lighter's flame.

I listened to threats of how father would sue and/or blow up the gas company's persons and premises. During this tirade, the pie was still in the oven and browning nicely.

When it was eventually served, it smelled distinctly of burnt forelock and facial hair. We abandoned the pie in preference to toasted York ham and English mustard sandwiches and another bottle of fine wine.

I did get to taste the pie at the Escoffier dinner, but that's another story.

CHICKEN PIES

Deep dish chicken pie with mushrooms Serves 4–6

Ingredients

1.5 kg (3 lb) chicken pieces

salt and pepper

plain flour

90 g (3 oz) butter

1 onion, sliced

1 cup chicken stock

1 cup dry white wine

3 slices bacon, lightly fried and cut into pieces

3 hard-boiled eggs, sliced

250 g (8 oz) mushroom caps, sliced

1 tablespoon chopped parsley

½ quantity puff pastry (see page 10) or 2–3 sheets ready-made pastry

1 egg, slightly beaten

3 tablespoons medium dry sherry

Method

Remove as many of the bones as possible from the chicken pieces. You can use them to make the chicken stock.

Coat the chicken pieces with salt, pepper and flour and sauté in the heated butter until lightly browned all over.

Add the onion, chicken stock and white wine and simmer, covered, for 40–45 minutes. Lift out the chicken pieces and put them into a deep pie dish.

Thicken the remaining liquid with a little flour. Blend the flour into a paste with water first.

Arrange the bacon pieces, egg slices and mushrooms over the chicken and lightly season with salt, pepper and the parsley. Pour the chicken sauce over this mixture.

Roll out the pastry to fit the pie dish. Lay it over the top of the pie and press onto the edge of the dish. Brush with beaten egg, then cut several steam vents in the pastry.

Bake in the oven at 230°C (450°F) for 10 minutes, then reduce the heat to 200°C (400°F) and bake a further 15–20 minutes.

Take the pie from the oven and, using a small funnel, drizzle the dry sherry through the steam holes. Let the pie stand for 10 minutes, then serve.

Peter's stuffed chicken breasts in rice paper

Serves 4

Ingredients

4 chicken fillets

a little butter

1 cup grated tasty cheese

3 spring onions, finely chopped

2 Granny Smith apples, peeled, cored and grated

1 carrot, peeled and grated

1 teaspoon grated fresh ginger

1 teaspoon chopped basil

Tabasco Sauce

4 sheets rice paper

black pepper

Method

Flatten chicken fillets out with a rolling pin, but don't hit them too hard or they'll split. Melt a little butter in a large pan and cook each chicken fillet until it changes colour. Remove from pan and dry with paper towel.

Mix together cheese, spring onions, apple and carrot and put a quarter of the mixture onto each fillet. Add a little ginger, basil and one drop of sauce to each fillet, then roll up each fillet.

Next, roll each fillet up in a piece of rice paper and season with pepper. Heat a little oil in a pan and quickly cook the chicken for a couple of minutes on each side. (All this must be done quickly so the rice paper does not go soggy.) Serve immediately with steamed fresh vegetables.

P.S. You can buy rice paper at most good supermarkets or food ingredient stores.

Fish pies

> The Admiral, the 'pinkers' and the pie

I remember my father inviting the Admiral of the Fleet along with one or two of his Commanders to partake of one of the old boy's pies.

'Pinkers', translated as pink gin and tonic, were prepared by stewards on loan from the naval establishments which proliferated in certain streets in Sydney. Around these spots, grown men, in shorts of the type I wore when I was a boy, could be seen striding vigorously up and down.

My old man bobbed around the naval establishments like a cork on a windswept sea, and the day of which I write was windswept. One of his particular pals was a Rear-Admiral. He arrived with his entourage promptly at the appointed time, but my pater was still under the shower. They were ushered into the lounge where my father's girlfriend was ensconced; a fluffy bikini-clad Norwegian lass who didn't seem to understand the proprieties of our English dominated morality.

But the navy men, being men of the world, took it in their stride and treated the unusual welcoming with some pleasure. The stewards, whom they had supplied, indulged them by rolling bitters judiciously around the inside of crystal goblets to capture the delicate pinks of the bitters before swirling gin and tonic into the glass.

The Admiral, the 'pinkers' and the pie

It was smooth sailing until the old boy burst through the forward door, completely naked except for a towel which he clasped in his left hand.

'Good God!' he ejaculated. 'Has the bloody party started? I've only just dried myself. But carry on without me, for I'll be with you well before the next bells.'

True to his word he arrived only minutes later, dressed in grey slacks, a white turtleneck sweater and a yachting jacket emblazoned with the seal of a retired sub-mariner of the Royal British Navy.

It was obvious that he'd had a few 'pinkers' under the shower as his mood was exuberant and jolly.

'Let's launch the bloody pie!' he shouted exuberantly. 'And let's do it in style,' he continued, waving a bottle of champagne as if he was about to smash it across the bow of the pie dish.

A mob of matelots moved into the room producing pies which

The Admiral, the 'pinkers' and the pie

puffed their puff pastry out as importantly as a politician's paunch.

'Good God!' gasped one of the guests. 'Surely the old bugger's not going to serve a humble pie. For God's sake, the Admiral's aboard.'

And it was the Admiral who struggled to his feet and called the crew to attention.

'God save the Queen,' he toasted her. 'And Her Majesty's ships and all those that sail in them.'

Glasses were clinked and emptied as the pies were cut and served.

'Nothing like a pie!' boomed the Admiral. 'Second to the Royal Navy, the pie united the Empire. Why,' he exclaimed, 'we coloured the map red as if we were spreading tomato sauce over one of our home-baked pies.'

Later that evening as the party was breaking up and the Admiral was congratulating the old boy on a fine performance, the Admiral added, 'You said you would like a berth on one of our ships going back to the motherland. We have one leaving next week if you would care to be aboard her.'

'My jolly word!' roared the old boy. 'I'll be there with bloody bells on.' And so it was settled. The following week the old man arrived at Naval Headquarters with enough baggage to outdo Zsa Zsa Gabor.

'My God!' gasped his friend, the Admiral. 'We've no room to stow that lot away.'

'And why not?' asked my father. 'You told me we were going on the latest vessel commissioned by the Navy.'

'And so we are,' ventured the brass. 'And there she is,' he continued, pointing his podgy finger at the sleek lines of HMS *Tactician*, the Royal Navy's latest submarine.

'I'm claustrophobic,' choked the old man swooning. Nevertheless he was bundled on board, but only after he insisted on retaining at least one suitcase.

FISH PIES

The Admiral's pie

Ingredients for an individual pie

½ cup celery, finely chopped

½ small Spanish onion, finely diced

a pinch of grated ginger

juice of 1 clove of garlic

white pepper

celery salt

125 g (4 oz) raw fillet of swordfish

½ cup cold, cooked, mashed potato

dash sour cream

squeeze of lemon juice

1 sheet of ready-made puff pastry

Method

Combine the celery, onion, ginger, garlic, pepper and salt in a bowl.

Roughly chop the swordfish and add it to the mixture.

Fold in the potato. Beat the lemon juice into the sour cream, then fold it in too. The mixture should now be the consistency of thick, clotted cream.

Spoon it into an individual pie dish. Alternatively, multiply the recipe by a factor of 4, so the pie can be shared by family or friends. Use a large ovenproof dish in this case.

Top the pie with the puff pastry. Cook it in a hot oven at 200°C (400°F) for 15–20 minutes until it's golden brown.

FISH PIES

Eel pie Serves 6–8

Ingredients

2 shallots or small onions, sliced

a little butter

1 dessertspoon chopped parsley

pinch of nutmeg

salt

freshly ground black pepper

2 wineglasses sherry

2 eels, skinned and chopped into 2.5 cm (1") pieces

cornflour

2 tablespoons lemon juice

2 hard-boiled eggs, quartered

1½ quantity puff pastry (see page 10) or 375 g ready-made puff pastry

Method

Fry the shallots in a little butter, add the chopped parsley, nutmeg, salt, pepper and sherry. After 5 minutes cooking, put the eel in and add sufficient water to cover. Bring to the boil and then simmer for 30 minutes.

Lift out the eel and thicken the stock with cornflour mixed with a little water. Add the lemon juice and cook for a few more minutes.

Arrange the eel in a pie dish with the quartered hard-boiled eggs. Pour over the sauce and set aside until cold.

Cover with puff pastry and bake in the oven at 200°C (400°F) for 20 minutes, then lower to 180°C (350°F) and cook for another 40 minutes.

FISH PIES

Fish pie Serves 2

Ingredients

250 g (8 oz) cooked, flaked fish

250 g (8 oz) mashed potato

30 g (1 oz) softened butter

1 egg, beaten

salt

freshly ground black pepper

a little butter

2 tablespoons fried breadcrumbs

Method

Combine the flaked fish with the mashed potato, softened butter and beaten egg, and season well with salt and pepper.

Put into a buttered pie dish, cover with the browned breadcrumbs, dot with butter and bake in the oven at 190°C (375°F) for 20 minutes or until golden brown.

Fresh oyster tart Serves 6

Pastry

Ingredients

1 teaspoon salt

10 g (½ oz) sugar

160 g (5 oz) butter

1 egg

1 tablespoon milk

250 g (8 oz) plain flour

Method

To make the pastry put the salt, sugar, butter (in small pieces), egg and milk into an electric mixer. Beat for a few seconds, then add the flour all at once. Beat until blended, then allow the dough to stand for at least an hour in the refrigerator.

Roll out the dough and line six tart shells 5 cm x 1 cm (2" x ½"). Trim off the excess.

Refrigerate the shells for one hour, then pop a circle of greaseproof paper into the bottom of each, and sprinkle rice on top of the paper to stop the pastry 'bubbling'.

Bake for 20 minutes in the oven at 200°C (400°F) until a pale golden brown. →

FISH PIES

Filling

Ingredients

2 eggs and 1 yolk

100 ml (3 fl oz) cream

200 ml (6 fl oz) fish stock

saffron powder

salt and pepper

Worcestershire Sauce

Tabasco Sauce

36 large oysters

chopped fresh chives to garnish

Method

Beat together the eggs and the extra egg yolk with the cream and fish stock. Add a pinch of saffron powder and then salt, pepper, and Worcestershire and Tabasco Sauces to taste.

Pop six oysters in each cooked pastry shell (first take out the paper and rice) and pour in the prepared filling mixture to almost fill each tart.

Bake in a pre-heated oven for 10 minutes at 230°C (450°F) until the filling is just set. Serve immediately, sprinkled with chives.

Perc's pie

To be pie-eyed is to be plastered, or so some say. Pie-eyed, to me, is to be a pie-ophile — one who not only sings the praise of the pie but also gobbles it down with glee at every available opportunity. I had such a friend: Perc the Pie Man.

Perc lived with his mother and his brother in a once salubrious suburb of a large Victorian country town. There he made his celebrated product. It was a freshwater fish pie further flavoured with carefully selected herbs and spices. Perc was well aware that the delicate flavour of freshwater fish needed to be coaxed onto the palate rather than smothered before it got there.

As you would imagine, Perc and his brother were fishermen. They could cast a fly with all the cunning and skill of an American cowboy casting his lariat to catch a break-away steer. In fact, Perc had been a trail blazer on the prairies of Wyoming before serving time as a marine at Guadalcanal, Iwo Jima and all those other areas of conflict which took so many young lives.

Perc was attracted to the mateship offered by Australians and liked being able to be in the bush, minutes from leaving the country town's suburbs.

He'd drive to commercial fish farms and load 44-gallon drums full of fish to be used for his pie fillings. The trout were kept alive on the journey home with oxygen pumped into the containers to ensure that the fish were as fresh as possible. This was necessary because, although Perc and his brother had fished the rivers and streams on the way to buy their bulk fish, they couldn't resist

Perc's pie

repeating the process on the way home. And that often meant an overnight stay in tents pitched on the banks of rivulets or dams.

At night, their freshly caught trout, redfin, or golden perch would be gutted then sprinkled with garlic salt, freshly ground pepper and tarragon leaves. Next they'd wrap the fish in paperbark dampened with white wine. The parcel would then be placed on the hot coals at the side of the brothers' camp fire. When the paperbark pies were considered ready, they were plucked from the coals, unwrapped and, using the bark as plates, the fish flesh was picked from the bones by eager fingers. Pannikins of white wine helped make the meal.

Perc's pie

Perc assured me that this was where he got the idea for his pies.

'When I went commercial, I knew I'd run out of paperbark,' laughed Perc. 'So I replaced it with pastry. And the good thing is, you get to eat the pastry. You still don't need a plate and you eat it in your fingers.'

I participated in one of these piscatorial adventures some months before Perc was tragically carried off to the great pie factory in the sky by a mysterious virus which attacked his heart.

We pitched our tents beside a clump of willows in which a flock of ibis were conducting an out-of-control noise convention. The sun had just started to dip when I made my first cast, which instantly wrapped itself around the willow fronds behind me. This caused great amusement among the members of the convention as well as the brothers. Spurning their advice to cut the line, I joined the birds on the willow branches which snapped, dropping me none too neatly into the eddies of the stream.

My belly-flop caused a mini-tidal wave to surf over a sand-bar where it deposited a glistening rainbow trout.

Regardless of the ignominity I was forced to suffer over the method used to catch my fish, I cooked it and ate it with relish (by 'relish' I mean 'delight', not the spicy mixture served with some cold meats).

After Perc passed on, his brother and his mother abandoned the business and sadly went back to Wyoming. But not before they sprinkled the ashes of Perc and a pie over his favourite fishing hole.

Perc's pie recipe

Take the bones from a fresh trout in the fashion I have illustrated — one trout per one person's pie. Now, from your oven, take the shortcrust pastry which you have blind baked (page 15). Into this tip the trout, sprinkle it judiciously with garlic salt, freshly cracked black pepper and a few flicks of tarragon leaves. Pop on a lid of ready-made puff pastry, roughly trimmed. Brush with beaten egg, sprinkle with poppyseed to indicate that the bush flies have been about and cook in a hot oven at 230°C (450°F) for 20–25 minutes or until golden brown.

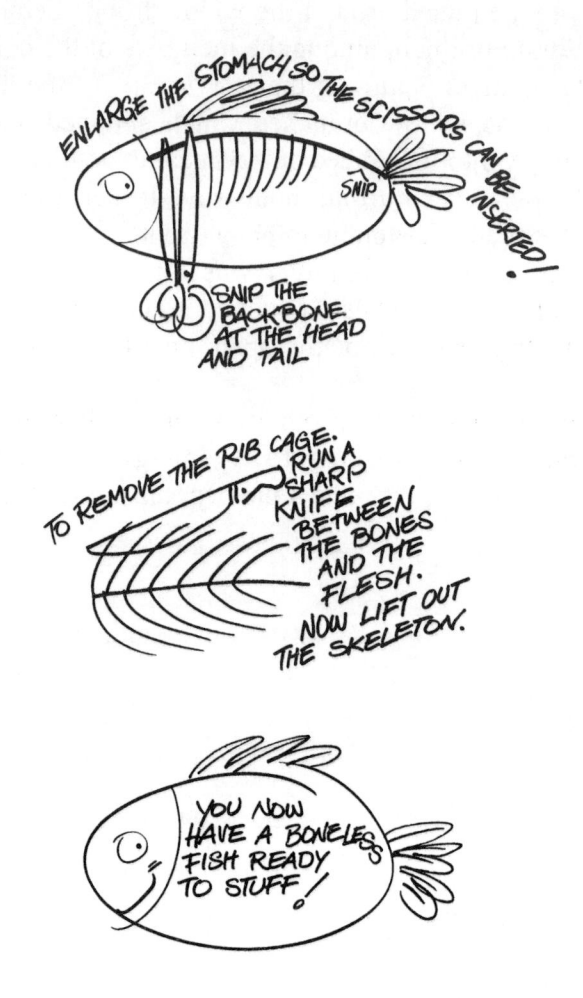

Pies with egg

Egg and bacon pie (quiche) Serves 4

Ingredients

½ quantity shortcrust pastry (see page 8)

4 eggs

¾ cup cream

3 rashers lean bacon, chopped

¾ cup chopped, dried, mixed fruit (apple, apricots, pears, etc)

½ cup grated tasty cheese

½ teaspoon dried mustard

¼ teaspoon mace

Method

Roll out the pastry. Line a 20 cm (8") flan dish leaving a 2.5 cm (1") overhang. Cover the pastry with a bit of greaseproof paper and pop some dried beans or rice on it.

Let it stand for 20 minutes in case it shrinks. Trim the pastry and leave a 1 cm (½") overhang. Pop it into the oven for 10 minutes at 200°C (400°F). Take it out and remove the paper and the beans or rice.

Prick the pastry all over with a fork, then return the case to the oven at 180°C (350°F) for another 20 minutes.

Now gently beat three of the eggs with the cream, stir in the bacon, half the fruit, all the cheese and the mustard.

In the cooked pastry case, make a ring of fruit. Break the remaining egg into the centre of the circle of fruit.

Spoon a bit of the mixture over the circle of the egg and fruit, then gently pour in the rest of the mixture.

Sprinkle with the mace, pop the pie into the oven to bake at 190°C (375°F) for 30 minutes. Eat it either hot or cold.

PIES WITH EGG

Spinach pie (spanakopita) Serves 6

Ingredients

1 kg (2 lb) spinach

1 cup chopped spring onions

1 tablespoon olive oil

1 cup cottage cheese

1 cup crumbled Fetta cheese

¼ cup grated Parmesan cheese

1 teaspoon dried basil leaves

4 eggs, lightly beaten

2 tablespoons chopped parsley

½ teaspoon nutmeg

freshly ground black pepper

6 rashers bacon, diced

10 sheets filo pastry

a little more olive oil for brushing pastry

extra egg, beaten

1 teaspoon poppyseeds

2 tins flat anchovies

Method

Cut the stems off the spinach and throw them into your stock pot. Then wash and coarsely shred the spinach. Cover and steam for 8 minutes in a metal colander over boiling water, then drain off all the moisture and leave to cool in a bowl.

Gently fry the onions in oil, add them to the spinach and stir in the cheeses, basil, eggs, parsley, nutmeg, freshly ground black pepper and bacon.

Line an ovenproof dish with 5 sheets of filo, brushing each sheet with oil (use a pastry brush).

Spread the filling on top of the filo. Brush and moisten the edges of the pastry with the other beaten egg, and pop the remaining pastry on top, again brushing each sheet including the top layer with oil.

Tuck the pastry into the side of the dish. Sprinkle it with poppyseeds and pop it into the oven to cook at 230°C (450°F) for 25 minutes or until the pastry is golden brown.

Take out the pie and make a pattern on top with the anchovies. Let it stand for 5 minutes before serving.

Cauliflower, carrot and Parmesan quiche Serves 4

Ingredients

½ quantity shortcrust pastry (see page 8)

1½ cups grated Parmesan cheese

1½ cups coarsely chopped fresh cauliflower

½ cup julienne of carrot

3 eggs

1½ cups cream

salt

hot pepper sauce

Method

Blind bake the pastry in a 23 cm (9") flan dish (see page 15).

Cook the cauliflower and carrot until they are just tender. Drain thoroughly.

Sprinkle half the cheese into the base of the pastry case. Add cauliflower and carrot keeping about ten pieces of carrot for later decoration. Sprinkle remaining cheese on top of the vegetables.

Lightly beat the eggs, stir in the cream, add salt and pepper sauce to taste and pour over the vegetables. Decorate with the pieces of carrot.

Bake in the oven at 150°C (300°F) for about 30 minutes until the top is lightly browned and the custard set. If the pastry edge starts to get too brown, cover with foil until the cooking is completed.

Let the quiche stand for 15 minutes at room temperature before cutting into wedges and serving.

PIES WITH EGG

Quick crust quiche Serves 4

Base

Ingredients

3 tablespoons butter, melted

½ cup crushed savoury biscuits

½ cup rolled oats

2 tablespoons grated Parmesan cheese

Method

Combine base ingredients and press into the bottom of a lightly buttered 20 cm (8") springform pan or flan tin. Bake at 190°C (375°F) for 10 minutes.

Cook the bacon in a non-stick pan until crisp, then quickly cook all the vegetables.

Combine bacon and vegies with the remaining ingredients and spoon into the prepared crust. Bake at 190°C (375°F) for 40–45 minutes or until set. Allow the quiche to cool a little before serving.

Filling

Ingredients

3 rashers bacon, chopped

1 carrot, grated

2 zucchini, grated and squeezed to remove moisture

1 cup sliced mushrooms

2 sticks celery

2 cups shredded Cheddar cheese

2 eggs, beaten with 1 cup milk

Onion pie Serves 4

Pastry

Ingredients

250 g (8 oz) plain flour

pinch salt

100 g (3 oz) unsalted butter

1 egg

1 tablespoon milk

1 egg white, beaten

Filling

Ingredients

50 g (1½ oz) butter

50 g (1½ oz) kaiserfleisch, finely chopped

410 g (13 oz) onions, finely sliced

salt and pepper to taste

35 ml (1 fl oz) milk

35 ml (1 fl oz) cream

1 bay leaf

few parsley stalks

4 eggs

2 tablespoons finely chopped parsley

Method

Rub the butter into the flour and salt until the mixture looks like fine breadcrumbs. Add the egg and enough milk to bring the dough together. Knead lightly and let it rest for 30 minutes.

Roll out to fit a 23 cm (9") tart dish. Trim off the overhanging pastry and prick all over. Leave for another 30 minutes before blind baking at 180°C (350°F) for 15 minutes. It should not brown. Let the pastry case cool, then brush the base with a lightly beaten egg white.

To make the filling, heat the butter over a very low heat and, with the pan covered, gently cook the kaiserfleisch and onion until the onion is soft (about an hour). Sprinkle with salt and pepper to taste, then put the mixture into a blender and purée.

Heat the milk and cream with the bay leaf and parsley stalks. Beat the eggs and pour over the hot milk, whisking continuously. Strain.

Mix the onion purée and hot custard together, taste and adjust the seasoning. Spoon into the prepared crust and scatter with parsley.

Bake at 180°C (350°F) for 25–30 minutes or until golden brown.

PIES WITH EGG

Peter's crunchy rice pie Serves 4

Base

Ingredients

1½ cups cooked brown rice

1 egg, lightly beaten

1 tablespoon lemon juice

½ teaspoon paprika

1 tablespoon finely chopped parsley

1 tablespoon toasted sesame seeds

Filling

Ingredients

250 g (8 oz) light cream cheese

2 tablespoons grated Parmesan cheese

2 eggs, lightly beaten

¾ cup milk

425 g (13½ oz) red or pink salmon, drained

¼ cup chopped spring onions

2 tomatoes, sliced

1 teaspoon dried basil

extra grated Parmesan cheese

Method

Combine all the ingredients for the base and mix well. Press into a 23 cm (9") pie dish and bake at 190°C (375°F) for 15 minutes.

Beat together cream cheese, Parmesan cheese, eggs and milk, mixing well. Stir in the salmon.

Pour this mixture into the rice crust, top with spring onions and tomato and sprinkle with basil and extra Parmesan cheese.

Bake at 180°C (350°F) for 45–50 minutes. Remove from oven and allow to stand 10 minutes before serving.

Vegetarian pies

> Television debut

When I decided to try my hand as a television person, I studied the medium.

'It's about communication,' I commented to my companion. 'If I can learn to master the art of communication, I've got half a chance of cracking it on the idiot box.'

Americans are great communicators, I thought. They have the gift of the gab as well as natural flair for entertainment. One has only to look at their success on the silver screen.

Mind you, the Poms were pretty good too but I reckoned the Aussie audience would want a bit more razzamatazz than the stoic, stiff upper lip of the Pommie thespians.

But it wasn't only the Hollywood hierarchy that I wished to emulate. In all sorts of promotional areas the Americans were masters. Take conventions for instance. As soon as the visiting firemen (as Americans call all convention delegates) had consumed their half a dozen dry martinis, a huge cake would be carried into the room. From the second or third tier of the cake would burst a scantily clad female who would then parade around the place blowing Marilyn Monroe kisses to the delegates, before being whisked away.

This was always a great success, so I thought why not have a go at it in Australia?

But we're not cake-eaters per se, so I had an enormous pie casing

Television debut

made, into which I placed my naked person. The instructions were that a gaggle of chefs would shoulder the pie, carry it into the television studio and plonk it before the cameras. I would burst through the pie's crust, hiding my scrotum behind a bottle of tomato sauce. Shooting navel high, the cameras would whirr and the show would be on.

But every time the chefs picked up the pie, I fell through the bottom of it. I quickly realised gimmicks were a pain in the bum, as well as learning the painful fact that pies were for eating not mucking around in.

And since at the time of that escapade I was working with the dairy industry, I created a Cheese Pie in honour of all Australia's dairy farmers and their contented cows.

Four different cheese pies

No. 1

On a sheet of puff pastry about 30 cm^2 (12" square), place a mound of loosely grated tasty cheese (same size as a cricket ball). Sprinkle the juice of three cloves of garlic — yes, three — a pinch of cayenne pepper, some pitted green olives, some thick threads of red capsicum and, for those who aren't vegetarians, some chopped eye of bacon. Pull the four corners of the pastry square over the filling and secure them. Ensure there are no openings in the pastry by pressing this swaggie bag of cheese in your hands. Twist the top of the pastry like a Hottentot's hairdo. Brush with beaten egg and pop the pie into a hot oven at 230°C (450°F) on a non-stick oven tray for 15 minutes.

No. 2

Do a similar thing with a different filling.

Par-cook some celery in boiling water. Take it out, let it cool, chop it and make a little mound. Mix in a quantity of grated cheese equal to the celery mound. Sprinkle on some caraway seed (some of my fine friends are averse to caraway seed and so I often make the same recipe but with a sprinkling of capers). Next add a sprinkle of coarsely ground black pepper and a good sprinkling of roughly chopped dates. The final ingredient is more grated tasty cheese. Add a mound of cheese, about half as big as the mound you have in front of you now. Place the mixture on a sheet of puff pastry and secure the parcel as in recipe No. 1. Cook as in No. 1 too.

No. 3

Combine equal quantities of grated tasty cheese and coarsely grated carrot. Add garlic juice to taste and a good sprinkle of black pepper. Chop up an apple and sprinkle it with lemon juice. Add a good sprinkle of sultanas, a good pinch of allspice and another handful of grated tasty cheese mixed with some grated Parmesan. Use a sheet of puff pastry secured and cooked as per No. 1.

VEGETARIAN PIES

No. 4 — Peter's cheese 'n vegetable pie Serves 4

Ingredients

2 onions, finely chopped

olive oil

1 cup cooked, mashed potato

1 cup cooked, mashed carrot

2 cups cooked, mashed pumpkin

2 cups grated extra tasty cheese

2 tomatoes, roughly chopped

1 tablespoon tomato paste

2 zucchini, sliced

4 sheets ready-made puff pastry

⅓ cup grated Parmesan cheese

1 egg, beaten

extra Parmesan cheese

Method

Cook the onion in a little oil until tender.

Add half the onion to the mashed vegetables and grated cheese and mix well. Add the remaining onion to the tomatoes, tomato paste and zucchini.

Using a 23 cm (9") flan tin, cut puff pastry into 4 × 25 cm (10") circles. Take one round, sprinkle with Parmesan cheese and place on a foil-lined oven tray. Place a second round on top. Place the pumpkin mixture onto the centre of the pastry leaving a 2.5 cm (1") border around the edge. Top with the tomato mixture.

Cut each of the remaining two sheets of pastry into 8 wedges. Brush edges of wedges with water and overlap, covering the vegetable filling. Brush the pastry with egg and sprinkle with Parmesan cheese.

Bake at 190°C (375°F) for 50–55 minutes or until golden brown. Serve hot or cold.

Pumpkin

When I was a boy, I would have considered the words I'm about to write as heresy.

Pumpkin pie.

Now we know of course that pumpkin pie is not only good for you, it tastes terrific too. And so do a whole range of other vegetable pies.

No doubt, as my mother did, you were told to eat your greens. 'If you don't eat your vegetables, you don't get dessert,' children were scolded by their mothers. And so we succumbed and ate the soggy mess, whose colours had been bleached out, along with the vitamins and minerals. The English habit of hung, drawn and quartered finished off the recipient. Our vegetables were drowned, boiled and beaten to achieve the same sad result.

But, the Poms aside, most other countries have cooks who venerate the vegetable. They mix and match flavours and textures. They make a kaleidoscope of colour to entice even the most jaded palate. The American pumpkin pie and the Asian curry puffs and spring rolls underline my point. And, hopefully, after you've eaten some of my pies, you'll agree that vegetables can replace meat to make a marvellous meal.

The much-maligned Brussels sprout has been touted by Australian scientists as a weapon in the fight against cardiovascular disease and cancer. CSIRO scientists found, in a study of fruit and vegetables, that the often spurned, green-leafed sprout along with strawberries and, incidentally, a cup of tea have high anti-oxidant levels which help prevent several nasty diseases. CSIRO's Human

Pumpkin

Nutrition Division spokesperson said they had measured the naturally occurring anti-oxidant capacity of fruits and vegetables and we should be poking more down our throats, they admonish. But they're only giving us half the story. The other half is taste.

I agree that the majority of Australians don't like Brussels sprouts but, if they were cooked with honey, lemon juice and bacon, wrapped in a cardamom spiced pastry shell and served hot and golden brown, we'd get a different reaction.

Cauliflowers with orange segments and grated tasty cheese would be complemented by flaky pastry. Tomato, basil and lima beans or lentils with a gentle curry enhancement would also be helped by filo pastry.

When you run down the list of flavour combinations I've suggested, remember they're just that — suggestions. You may well want to subtract one fruit and replace it with a vegetable. (Tomatoes and pumpkin are fruit. In fact anything with pips is a fruit.) If one herb is too strong, replace it with one you prefer.

I'm sure you'll agree much of the fun of cooking is inventing flavours to suit yourself, your family and friends.

Sour cream–pumpkin pie Serves 8–10

Ingredients

1 quantity sweet shortcrust pastry (see page 8)

1 egg white, unbeaten

2 cups cooked pumpkin

2 whole eggs, slightly beaten

1 egg yolk

1 cup brown sugar

½ teaspoon ground ginger

½ teaspoon ground cinnamon

¼ teaspoon ground nutmeg

¼ teaspoon ground mace

½ cup milk

½ cup cultured sour cream

Method

Line a 23 cm (9") pie dish with pastry and flute the edges. Brush unbeaten egg white over the bottom. Chill in the freezer for 10 minutes.

Preheat the oven to 220°C (425°F).

Combine all the remaining ingredients, then beat with a rotary beater until smooth.

Pour into the chilled pie shell and bake for 10 minutes. Lower the temperature to 180°C (350°F) and continue baking for about 50 minutes until a knife inserted in the centre comes out clean.

Take it out of the oven, cool to room temperature, but don't chill.

VEGETARIAN PIES

My son's jumbo vegetable rolls Makes 9

Ingredients

1 cup cooked brown rice

½ cup corn kernels

½ cup peas

½ cup grated carrot

1 onion, finely chopped

1 stick celery, finely chopped

1 red capsicum, roughly chopped

200 g (6½ oz) soft cream cheese

1 cup grated tasty cheese

1 tablespoon fruit chutney

½ teaspoon chilli powder

3 sheets ready-made puff pastry

1 egg, lightly beaten

Method

Combine rice, vegetables, cheeses, chutney and chilli powder, mixing well.

Spoon mixture along the edge of each sheet of pastry. Roll up and cut each roll into three.

Place rolls on lightly floured oven tray and brush with egg. Bake at 200°C (400°F) for 30 minutes or until golden brown.

VEGETARIAN PIES

Chick pea pies (a Lebanese lenten specialty)

Makes 20

Ingredients

250 g (8 oz) chick peas

salt

15 g (½ oz) fresh yeast or 7 g (¼ oz) dried yeast

pinch of sugar

300 ml (10 fl oz) lukewarm water

500 g (1 lb) plain flour

1 teaspoon salt

2 tablespoons olive oil

Method

Soak the chick peas for a few hours. Boil in fresh water until tender (about 40 minutes), adding salt towards the end of the cooking. Drain and let them dry.

Dissolve the yeast with a pinch of sugar in about 150 ml (5 fl oz) of the lukewarm water. Leave aside in a warm place for about 10 minutes, or until the mixture begins to bubble.

Meanwhile sift the flour and salt into a large warmed mixing bowl. Make a well in the centre and add the oil, and the yeast mixture. Work the dough vigorously, adding the remaining lukewarm water gradually to make a soft dough.

Knead for about 15 minutes until the dough is pliable and elastic and comes away from the sides of the bowl.

Cover with a damp cloth and set aside in a warm place for 2–3 hours or until doubled in bulk. To prevent a dry crust forming on the surface, put a very little oil in the bottom of the bowl and roll the ball of dough in it, to coat the entire surface before leaving it to rest.

Divide the dough into twenty small lumps. Flatten them out and cut into rounds with a pastry cutter. →

VEGETARIAN PIES

Place on oiled trays and press a handful of chick peas into the centre of each pie. Bake at 180°C (350°F) for 20–30 minutes until cooked and slightly coloured. They should be eaten warm.

Leek and goat cheese tarts Makes 4–6

Pastry

Ingredients

- 90 g (3 oz) plain flour
- 3 tablespoons unsalted butter
- 150 g (5 oz) goat cheese
- 3 tablespoons sour cream

Filling

Ingredients

- 1 large or 2 small leeks, white part only
- 1 tablespoon butter
- pepper
- nutmeg
- 2 eggs
- ¾ cup cream

Method

Combine the pastry ingredients into a dough. Refrigerate one hour. Roll thinly and line four pastry moulds (or more depending on the mould size). You can use shallow muffin tins.

Cut greaseproof paper to size, lay it on the pastry and weight with dry beans. Bake in the oven at 200°C (400°F) for 12–15 minutes. Remove the beans.

Wash and finely slice the leeks. Lightly sauté in the butter and season with pepper and nutmeg. Divide between the pastries.

Make a custard by combining the eggs and the cream. Pour it gently into the tart shells.

Return the tarts to the oven for 10–15 minutes until set.

VEGETARIAN PIES

Potatoes in a pastry shell Serves 6

Ingredients

5 large baked potatoes

⅓ cup melted butter

¼ cup cream

½ cup finely chopped parsley

3 cloves garlic, crushed

1 teaspoon dried mixed herbs

salt

freshly ground pepper

1 quantity of puff pastry (see page 10) or use ready-made pastry

1 egg, beaten

Method

Scoop the potato flesh out of each shell and put it into a large bowl. Add the melted butter, cream, parsley, garlic and herbs. Blend gently with a fork; don't mash it. Season with salt and pepper.

Divide the pastry into two pieces. Roll out pastry to 3 mm (⅛") thickness and cut out a 23 cm (9") circle. Pop it onto an oiled baking tray. Mound the potatoes in the centre of the pastry leaving a 1.5 cm (½") pastry border.

Roll out the other half and cut out a 26 cm (10½") circle. Put it over the top of the potatoes, pressing the edges of the pastry firmly together. Fold the bottom edge over the top pressing firmly to seal tightly. Pat top to flatten.

Brush the top of the pie with beaten egg. Make three slashes in the top with a sharp knife and bake in the oven at 200°C (400°F) for about 25 minutes until golden brown.

Cut into wedges and serve.

My Dad's vegetable pasties Serves 4

Ingredients

1 onion, finely chopped

olive oil

1 cup cooked, diced potato

½ cup cooked, diced carrot

½ cup cooked corn kernels

½ cup peas

1 tablespoon corn relish

2 tablespoons finely chopped parsley

2 cups grated tasty cheese

3 sheets ready-made shortcrust pastry

1 egg, beaten

Method

Cook the onion in a little oil until tender. Add the vegetables and cook for 5 minutes. Add the remaining ingredients.

Divide each sheet of pastry into four squares. Place ⅓ cup of mixture into the centre of each square. Fold in the four corners to form a parcel.

Place pasties onto a lightly floured baking tray and brush with egg. Bake at 220°C (425°F) for 20–25 minutes. Serve hot or cold.

VEGETARIAN PIES

Pasties with vegetable coulis Serves 4

Ingredients

12 mini pasties (see page 105)

a selection of vegetables; about 3 cups when chopped

2 tablespoons olive oil

good pinch marjoram

freshly ground black pepper

a little chicken stock, if needed

¼ cup cream

½ cup grated tasty cheese

watercress for garnish

Method

Peel and chop the vegetables. Heat the olive oil in a large heavy frying pan and add the vegetables. Sprinkle them with marjoram and pepper and cook until they are soft.

Put them into a blender and purée them. If necessary, add a little chicken stock to make it easier to purée.

Pour the purée into a saucepan and stir in the cream.

Heat the pasties. Spoon a quarter of the vegetable coulis onto a heatproof plate and spread it out to form a circle. Place the pasties in the middle of the plate and sprinkle the cheese on top of the pasties.

Put the plate under the grill until the cheese is melted, then serve decorated with a sprig of fresh watercress.

Baked beans

'Tinned baked beans are barbarous,' barked a dogmatic gourmet mate of mine. 'The red sauce they sink them in is hideous. The beans themselves are mushy and without flavour. Eating them is like attempting to chew glue made from flour and water. A pox on them and all those who can them.'

Mind you, he canned them faster and more furiously than the automated lines that spew the beans into their tin coffins.

I dared not admit to my fine-palated friend that I occasionally serve baked beans, much to the enjoyment of my family and friends.

Oh, I agree with much of what my companion said: the sauce is vile, but easily washed off; the beans *are* mushy, but nowhere as mushy as mashed potatoes which, I'm sure, most of us adore. Their flavour, like potatoes, is not overpowering and therefore welcomes companion flavours such as garlic and/or onions, herbs and spices and an array of other palate-pleasing additions. Try the sauce I've concocted to marry mashed potatoes and the baked beans.

Start with a tin of baked beans — ring-pull of course. Empty them into a colander and rinse away the sauce my friend finds so offensive. Sprinkle the beans with a little garlic salt and some cracked pepper. Take the skin off two tomatoes: hold the tomatoes on a fork over a gas flame until the skin bursts and peels away easily. You can also skin tomatoes by putting them in boiling water but this takes a little longer.

Now mash the skinless tomatoes until they are pulp. Squeeze the juice of a lemon over them and a few squirts of soy sauce. Add a finely chopped onion and the juice of four cloves of garlic. Sprinkle

Baked beans

this mixture with half a cup of finely chopped parsley and stir in the beans.

Now, fold some mashed potato, that has been softened with knobs of butter or a light olive oil, into the bean mixture.

Lay out five sheets of filo pastry and interleave them with grated tasty cheese. Pop enough of the mixture onto the centre of the pastry so that you can easily fold the pastry over the bean mixture to form a square.

Turn the parcel upside down so it cannot unwrap. Brush the top with a beaten egg and pop it into a hot oven at 220°C (425°F) until the pastry is golden brown.

This recipe is dedicated to my dear friend, Ric Otton, who is one of the world's great baked bean eaters.

Pizza Pies

A pizzeria is a type of simple eating house in southern Italy where a quick, small meal is served. Usually it's a pizza but not necessarily. These institutions have spread to northern Italy as well as most cities throughout the world. Look out of your window and you'll probably see one. And these pizzerias serve pies, because 'pizza' means 'pie' in Italian. But in its more primitive form, pizza is a round of yeast dough spread with tomatoes and Mozzarella cheese and baked in a very hot oven.

The most famous of the pizzas is the Neapolitan Pizza and it is very substantial. Actually, there are enough variations in pizza-making to fill this complete book and another library of the same. For instance, the Roman Pizza is cheese, onions but no tomato. The Ligurian Pizza has onions, black olives and anchovies. Practically every region in Italy lays claim to a unique pizza topping. So, too, does the shape of pizzas vary between various regions. Some are round like most of those made in Australia, some are square, some are oblong or oval.

I have listed a series of thought starters for you. But remember, your pizza topping is limited only by your imagination or the availability of the foods.

Cheesy ideas

It would seem nigh impossible in Australia to purchase a pizza without one of its ingredients being cheese. Mind you, I'm a great cheese eater but I'm not an advocate for cheese as an essential ingredient in everything we eat. And, for goodness sake, why don't our pizza producers offer a variety of cheeses? I'm sure the mozzarella industry would be brought to its knees if the pizzerias decided they had grated their last knob of stringy yellow stuff.

PIZZA PIES

Here are some alternative cheeses for pizzas.

- Stracchino, with its marvellous, sharp flavour and soft texture, marries marvellously with cooked quince and moist pork.
- Shaved Romano with swordfish, tomato and olives.
- A tasty cheese grated with nothing more than oregano, garlic, black pepper and freshly grated lemon rind.
- Mixing cheeses is also marvellous for a pizza top. Grated Parmesan, Cheddar and wafers of Havarti mixed with spinach leaves and bacon, garlic juice and finely sliced Spanish onion will also make a magnificent topping to pizza dough.
- Try soft blue cheese spread over the pizza base, then topped with finely diced emu meat, chunked tomato and zucchini.
- A mixture of creamed mashed potato, diced raw onion, grated Cheddar and Romano topped with sliced, moist turkey breast and mango, sprinkled with black pepper and chopped green olives.
- Rabbit and radicchio spiced with shaved Romano.
- Duck, avocado and Fetta.
- Quail, hoy sin sauce with a touch of plum sauce dotted with small cubes of Bocconcini.

But, folks, you can delete the cheese from any of my suggestions and I am confident you would still be intrigued and delighted by the results.

Simplicity in any marrying of flavours is what has created many of the great dishes of the past. Too often we feel the necessity to fling something else in or on 'just in case'.

Paul Bocuse once told me 'Take out as many ingredients from a recipe as you can without altering the flavour and I would be impressed.' He went on to explain, jabbing his rigid finger at a series of ingredients listed in a recipe book he had opened in his library, 'The fellow who wrote this didn't seem to understand that that herb counteracts that flavour, and that one nullifies that. Get rid of all of them and we would be able to taste the veal that God has gone to so much trouble to have made available for us.'

'Never send a simple soul to cook a simple meal,' another famous chef once advised me. It's the clever cook who can simplify foods so you can identify the flavours you are being offered.

Many of our pizzas in Australia are complicated concoctions served as a kaleidoscope of colour which would put Blue Poles to shame. Nevertheless, many of my acquaintances I'm sure would disagree with me. 'A pizza,' I can hear them squeal, 'must be a mass of flavours, otherwise we're back to roast lamb and three veg.'

I shall make no further comment other than to say that one of the most marvellous pizzas I have eaten was simply topped with softened skinless tomato and flaked, moist, smoked trout. It was sprinkled with extra virgin olive oil; drizzled with adequate garlic juice; and seasoned with black pepper. It was heated, but not fiercely. To die for.

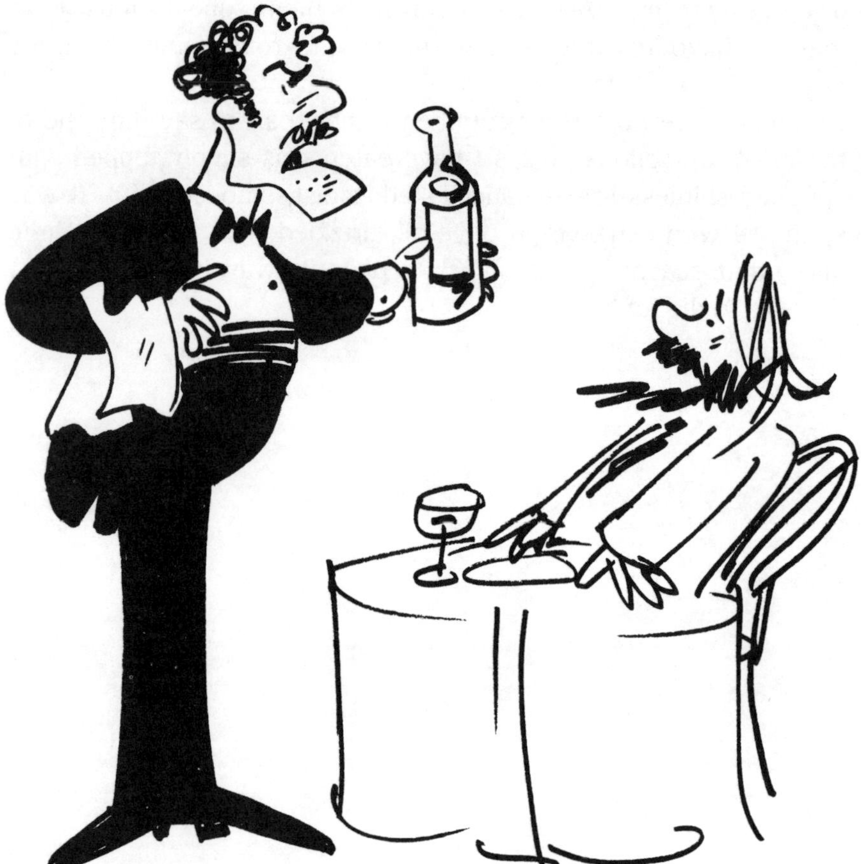

No cheese please!

As a young man I travelled to Venice and Florence. At the open-air roof restaurant of Venice's Excelsior Danielle I ordered a bottle of burgundy and a pizza to accompany it. I asked for a topping of thick slices of raw tomato sprinkled with garlic salt and a little wine vinegar, a goodly smattering of plump mussels and cooked artichoke hearts.

'Which cheese would you like?' asked the waiter.

'No cheese, but some freshly ground black pepper.'

'Why do you not want cheese? Have you a cholesterol problem?'

'No. I wish a plate of Gorgonzola and crisp toast to follow.'

'I understand. But why should that preclude you from having, say, Bocconcini with this pizza?'

'I don't wish two cheeses in the same meal.'

'But that's nonsense,' said the waiter. 'A normal cheese platter has more than one cheese on it and, if you don't wish to eat too much cheese, simply have small pieces of many rather than a lot of one.'

'I don't want the bloody cheese on the pizza, pal,' I snapped.

'You're Australian, am I right?' he replied with a knowing sneer. 'They have no conception of cheese.'

'Listen, mate,' I snarled. 'We make better cheese than any of the muck your mates make.'

'Made from the recipes you've pinched from us,' he replied haughtily. 'Now would you like shaved Romano on the mussels? After all, it's not a full fat cheese like the Froggies' Camembert.'

I looked at him pleadingly, but before I could answer he said,

No cheese please!

'Right. That's settled. Do you want to taste the burgundy or shall I pour it, which is what most of you Australians insist on.'

I was too weakened by the exchange to reply.

He took my sulk as an affirmative and splashed the wine into the glass, expertly twisting the bottle so no drip would spot the snow-white drapery.

Whilst I ate the magnificent pizza he kept glancing at me to ensure I wasn't flicking the wafer thin shaves of cheese onto the carpet.

I finished and was wiping my lips with the serviette when he materialised at the table, beaming, 'You obviously enjoyed it. Was it not perfect?'

'It was delightful, and I noted that you included a little onion. But you should have either taken the salt from the cheese or not used

No cheese please!

the garlic salt. Therefore I shall tip neither you nor your chef,' I smiled, giving him the exact amount of money that his bill of fare asked for.

'But you have, my young Aussie,' he replied gaily, sweeping my notes onto his tray.

'It's not stated on the bill,' I snapped.

'Then maybe I'm only teasing you,' he laughed.

I bloody well knew he wasn't but dignity and a strict upbringing did not allow me to thump him and, after all, the pizza was very nearly perfect.

The next morning I flew to Florence where I was amazed to see a spaghetti pizza. On a delightful summer's evening I was swept through the narrow, arched alleyways by a tidal wave of tourists. The churches were nearly outnumbered by the pizzerias. The recipes ranged from the classic to the absurd. The Spaghetti Pizza was simply a Bolognaise on a pizza base. And, by golly, it was good. I had ordered it in disbelief, but imagine the best Spaghetti Bolognaise you've ever eaten simply sat atop a crusty base. It was, indeed, good-o. Nevertheless I had thoughtfully ordered only a sliver and therefore was able to indulge in all the other myriad mixtures which were set out to tantalise the palates of the passers-by.

Here is a pot-pourri of what I ate, on what I insist was a fact-finding mission.

PIZZA PIES

Tuscan pizza

Ingredients

3 cups self-raising flour, sifted

¼ cup grated Parmesan cheese

1¼ cups milk

½ cup tomato paste

125 g (4 oz) shredded ham

1 egg, lightly beaten

¼ cup chopped fresh parsley

250 g (8 oz) Mozzarella cheese slices

Method

Combine flour and Parmesan cheese in a bowl. Make a well in the centre of the dry ingredients and add milk. Mix to a soft dough.

Roll out into an oblong shape. Place on a lightly oiled oven tray.

Spread with tomato paste and top with ham, egg, parsley and Mozzarella slices.

Bake at 220°C (425°F) for 15–20 minutes or until cooked.

Potato pizza

Ingredients

1.5 kg (3 lb) potatoes, peeled and chopped

¼ cup olive oil

freshly ground black pepper

1 cup shredded Mozzarella cheese

45 g (1½ oz) anchovy fillets, drained and chopped

3 tomatoes, roughly chopped

2 rashers lean bacon, chopped

1 teaspoon dried oregano

Method

Cook potatoes until tender and mash with olive oil and pepper.

Lightly oil a 35 cm (14") pizza tray and spread the potato mixture over it.

Sprinkle with Mozzarella and anchovy fillets. Cover with tomato, bacon and oregano.

Drizzle with a little extra oil and bake at 200°C (400°F) for 30 minutes.

PIZZA PIES

Chilli mini pizzas

Ingredients

3 sheets ready-made puff pastry

⅓ cup tomato paste

½ red capsicum, finely chopped

310 g (10 oz) cooked red kidney beans

1 small red chilli, finely chopped

1 spring onion, finely chopped

2 cups shredded Mozzarella cheese

Method

Cut pastry into rounds with a 6 cm round cutter. Spread with tomato paste.

Combine red capsicum, kidney beans, chilli, spring onion and Mozzarella. Mix until well combined.

Spoon onto pastry rounds.

Bake at 220°C (425°F) for 10–15 minutes or until cheese is golden brown.

Vegetarian pizza

Ingredients

2 cups self-raising flour, sifted

1 teaspoon dried oregano

⅓ cup olive oil

1 egg, lightly beaten

½ cup milk

½ cup Italian style spicy tomato sauce

2 cups reduced fat shredded Mozzarella cheese

¼ cup black olives, sliced and stones removed

½ cup cooked corn kernels

½ cup sliced mushrooms

1 medium green capsicum, thinly sliced

½ cup pineapple pieces

Method

Combine flour and oregano in a bowl. Stir in the oil, egg and milk. Mix lightly to form a soft dough.

Roll out dough into a 28 cm (11") circle and place on a lightly oiled oven tray.

Spread with tomato sauce, top with Mozzarella and arrange olives, vegetables and pineapple on top.

Bake at 200°C (400°F) for 20 minutes.

PIZZA PIES

Pizza sandwich

Ingredients

2 large frozen pizza bases

⅓ cup Italian style tomato sauce

250 g (8 oz) Mozzarella cheese slices

4 slices ham

250 g (8 oz) cooked chopped spinach

2 tomatoes, thickly sliced

1 small onion, thinly sliced

1 tablespoon finely chopped parsley

Method

Place one pizza base onto a lightly oiled oven tray. Bake at 220°C (425°F) for 10 minutes. Cool slightly.

Spread baked pizza base with tomato sauce. Layer with half the Mozzarella. Top with ham, spinach, tomato and remaining cheese.

Place the uncooked pizza base on top and press firmly around the edge of the pizza.

Sprinkle with onion and parsley. Bake at 200°C (400°F) for 20 minutes or until golden brown.

PIZZA PIES

Crusty pizza

Ingredients

500 g (1 lb) bread dough

¾ cup Italian style tomato sauce

1½ cups shredded Mozzarella cheese

1 cup halved artichoke hearts, drained

2 tablespoons chopped fresh basil

1 small onion, finely sliced

75 g (2½ oz) anchovy fillets, drained and chopped

½ cup olives, sliced and stones removed

½ cup shredded hot salami

Method

Roll dough to fit lightly oiled 35 cm (14") pizza tray. Cover dough with tomato sauce and Mozzarella.

Cover one half with artichokes, basil and sliced onion.

Cover the remaining half with anchovies, olives and salami.

Bake at 220°C (425°F) for 20 minutes or until lightly browned underneath.

Bread dough

Ingredients

30 g (1 oz) fresh yeast or 1 envelope dry yeast

½ cup warm water

500 g (1 lb) plain flour

Method

Dissolve the yeast in the warm water.

Heap the flour in a mound on a board, make a well in the centre and pour in the dissolved yeast. Add enough extra water to form a soft dough.

Knead until smooth and elastic. Cover with a towel and let rise in a large bowl until doubled in volume.

PIZZA PIES

Three-corner pizza

Ingredients

2 cups self-raising flour

1 teaspoon dried oregano

½ cup olive oil

1 egg, lightly beaten

½ cup milk

½ cup Italian style tomato sauce

1½ cups shredded Mozzarella cheese

⅓ cup sliced mushrooms

1 onion, sliced

¼ cup green capsicum, thinly sliced

2 slices ham, chopped

¼ cup chopped parsley.

Method

Combine flour and oregano in a mixing bowl. In another bowl, combine the olive oil, egg and milk and then stir it into the flour. Mix together well to form a soft dough.

Roll dough on a floured board into a 28 cm (11") circle. Place on a lightly oiled oven tray. Spread pizza base with tomato sauce. Top with cheese.

Cover one-third of the pizza with mushrooms and onion, one-third with capsicum and one-third with ham. Sprinkle with parsley.

Bake in oven at 240°C (475°F) for 10–15 minutes.

Thai pies

> **The mysterious curry puff**

It's marvellous, yet still a mystery, that most Thai restaurants serve the ubiquitous curry puff.

I order, and eat them, out of habit. Certainly not from a desire for the taste of Thailand for they are nothing more than mashed potatoes and not much else, wrapped in puff pastry.

Now I'm not against either potato or pastry but I do feel they both are accepted in the culinary world mainly because they are vehicles for other flavours.

Pastry entraps a mixture of other foods while the potato's bland flavour is ideal to marry with stronger, more pungent flavours. Therefore the thought of the curry puff is perfect; the pastry case, and the bland mashed potato to smooth and carry the curry. But somehow they forget the curry. Or, if it is included, it's as colourless and as gentle as a fairy's fart (breath).

There have been quite a few conspiracies in this world; the hiding of Elvis and Hitler in South America, Nixon's tapes, Fraser's trousers ... and ranking amongst the best of them is our Thai curry puff. There must be a huge hidden factory which produces them by the semi-trailer load for they are as common as Khaki Campbell ducks or pigeon poo in Trafalgar Square. But if I'm right, why is it so? Why don't these curry puff pie-makers come clean and let us know the game that is afoot?

We are all led to believe that the restaurants make the curry puffs in their own kitchens. And why they don't, I wouldn't know. It's very easy.

THAI PIES

How to assemble and cook a curry puff

Take a circle of puff pastry and place filling on one half of it. Brush the edges with oil or beaten egg, then fold the empty half of the pastry over the filling. Press the edges together and crimp them. Give the pot belly of the puff a brush with beaten egg, then cook it in a hot oven at 230°C (450°F) for about 15 minutes.

Classic puff filling

Begin by sprinkling some good Indian or Ceylonese curry powder into some oil. If you don't have powder but do have curry paste, pop in a modicum of that. Dice an onion finely and fry it in the oil. When the onion is soft, add grated sweet potato and finely chopped radish. Sprinkle with some garlic salt and add some chopped mixed nuts. Allow the mixture to go cold, then follow the procedure for assembling and cooking a curry puff (see above).

Variations

I have not included quantities in these recipes as I think it's fun to mix and match to suit your own palate. Also, I have considered the recipes as thought starters only. Patrons to whom I have served these mixtures have all been enthusiastic but then my clients are foodies and are interested in all manner of tastes from the subtle to the bizarre.

And talking of bizarre, I once ate a pie in a Turkish bazaar — both of which were, indeed, bizarre. But that's another story.

No. 1

Soften some thinly sliced zucchini in boiling water. Drain. Mix in an amount of cooked green peas and grated carrot equal to half the amount of zucchini. Sprinkle with some onion salt. Lightly wet a pan with sesame oil and sprinkle in some ground cumin, coriander and curry leaves. Stir in the mixture to coat it with oil, then allow it to go cold. Follow the procedure for assembling and cooking a curry puff (see above).

THAI PIES

No. 2

Mix together some mashed potato, corn kernels, grated fresh ginger, chopped walnuts and chopped spring onion. Sprinkle with some garlic salt. Bruise a stalk of lemongrass and drop it into some olive oil which you've warmed in a pan. Move the bruised grass around the pan to flavour the oil. Turn it over, then take it out and warm the potato mixture in the oil. Allow it to go cold then follow the procedure for assembling and cooking a curry puff (page 124).

No. 3

Soften parsnip by boiling it, then mash it. Mix in some eye of bacon, some chopped hard-boiled egg and a sprinkling of onion salt. Stir a small amount of sambal bajak into some oil and slightly warm the mixture in the oil. Allow it to go cold, then follow the procedure for assembling and cooking a curry puff (page 124).

No. 4

Cook and mash the flesh of a butternut pumpkin. Mix in some minced lean beef (uncooked) and some cooked lima beans and sprinkle with some garlic salt. Slightly warm this mixture in some macadamia oil flavoured with Jamaican curry powder (or Indian or Ceylonese depending on your preference). Allow it to go cold, then follow the procedure for assembling and cooking a curry puff (page 124).

No. 5

Soften some roughly chopped turnip in boiling water and mix it with the same quantity of mashed potato. Sprinkle liberally with coarsely cracked pepper and some onion salt. Mix in some diced Chinese sausage. Put some olive oil in a pan and warm a spoonful of hot lime pickle. Add the turnip mixture and warm slightly. Allow it to go cold, then follow the procedure for assembling and cooking a curry puff (page 124).

THAI PIES

No. 6

Mix some grated raw carrot and some cooked baked beans in the ratio of 2:1 (e.g 2 cups carrot to 1 cup beans). Sprinkle with garlic salt and freshly ground black pepper and add some chopped Weisswurst. Wet a pan with olive oil and flavour it with a sprinkle of dry curry powder. Pop the carrot mixture into the pan, being careful not to overcook either the carrot or the sausage. Allow it to go cold, then follow the procedure for assembling and cooking a curry puff (page 124).

No. 7

Mash some potato and smooth in a splash of cream and sweet butter. Mix in a scoop of prepared Dijon mustard. Sprinkle with some dried sultanas, some finely chopped fresh ginger, garlic juice and salt and pepper. Gently warm the mixture in some oil. Allow it to go cold, then follow the procedure for assembling and cooking a curry puff (page 124).

No. 8

Peel some tomatoes and roughly chop them. Sprinkle them with garlic salt and the juice from one or more garlic cloves. Add some freshly ground black pepper, a splash of soy sauce and a dob of fruit chutney. Mix it all together. Heat a good sprinkling of mustard seed and cottonseed oil in a pan. Add the mixture. Don't cook the tomato until it's sloppy; simply warm it so it holds its shape. Allow it to go cold, then follow the procedure for assembling and cooking a curry puff (page 124).

No. 9

Slice and dice some green and red capsicum. I use the seeds whereas most recipes suggest you throw them away — what a waste. Dice a Spanish onion and mix with the peppers as well as some cooked brown rice. Sprinkle liberally with paprika and a judicious flick of cayenne pepper. Crumble some crisped eye of bacon and stir it through. Warm a slivered clove of garlic in a pan of canola oil, add the mixture and heat until warm. Allow it to go cold, then follow the procedure for assembling and cooking a curry puff (page 124).

No. 10
Roughly dice an eggplant leaving the skin on. Pour puréed fresh tomato over the eggplant. Add finely chopped garlic and fresh ginger and a goodly sprinkle of coarse cracked pepper. Toss with diced softened Chinese mushrooms (soak them overnight to soften them). Sprinkle some dried English mustard into some hot olive oil, add the mixture and warm it through. Allow it to go cold, then follow the procedure for assembling and cooking a curry puff (page 124).

No. 11
Scramble some eggs. Begin by cracking each individual egg into a saucer to ensure its freshness. You don't want to crack six, seven or eight eggs into a bowl and find the ninth one not up to scratch and therefore do the lot in. So transfer the eggs one by one from the saucer to a bowl and mix in a little orange and lemon juice. For eight eggs, squeeze the juice of half a small lemon and the juice of a quarter of an orange. I know that's a wee bit difficult but, in other words, not much more orange juice than lemon. Once you've added the juice, sprinkle in garlic salt, some white pepper (black pepper being the wrong colour), a small scoop of cream and some dobs of butter. Gently mix it together.

Don't beat it furiously because you want the white and the yellow to be still definable. Drop in some chopped Spanish onion, some chopped parsley and some cooked green peas. Pour the mixture into a pan, liberally wet with melted butter and move the mixture around until it thickens. Be most careful that it doesn't dry out. Though the word 'sloppy' is not one that conjures up a pretty picture, it actually describes how the just-getting-solid mixture should be. Allow it to go cold, then follow the procedure for assembling and cooking a curry puff (page 124).

THAI PIES

No. 12

Cut up some cabbage and cook it in a pan with some oil along with some capers, the merest touch of cream, a generous squeeze of garlic juice, some freshly ground black pepper, diced salami and a pinch of some garam masala. When the cabbage begins to soften take it out of the pan and allow it to cool, then follow the procedure for assembling and cooking a curry puff (page 124).

No. 13

Wash a handful of spinach leaves, pat dry, then cut out the stems. Add the leaves to a pan with a little sesame oil, some garlic juice and chopped chives, and a sprinkle of chopped tarragon. Finely chop the stalks and add them to the pan. When the spinach leaves are wilted take the mixture out of the pan. Allow it to go cold. Smear a knob of soft blue cheese on a circle of puff pastry, then follow the procedure for assembling and cooking a curry puff (page 124).

No. 14

Add a coating of oil to a pan and drop in slivers of garlic, a handful of diced ham and some flowerets of cauliflower. Cut the stalks of the flowerets into thin medallions and add them too. Once the flowerets begin to soften, remove the mixture from the pan and allow it to go cold. Place the mixture on a circle of puff pastry and sprinkle with grated tasty cheese, then follow the procedure for assembling and cooking a curry puff (page 124).

No. 15

Fry some lean bacon, diced brown onion and slivers of garlic in a pan of olive oil. Roughly chop some Brussels sprouts and cook them until the leaves have softened. Sprinkle lightly with salt. Take the mixture from the pan and allow it go cold. Place a spoonful of it on a circle of pastry. Top it with a scoop of camembert cheese (without the rind), then follow the procedure for assembling and cooking a curry puff (page 124).

THAI PIES

No. 16

Splash some olive oil into a pan and fry some sliced and diced onion, and thin slivers of garlic. Add some shredded lettuce and sprinkle with a little salt. The lettuce softens quickly and when it has, remove the mixture and let it go cold. Whilst that is happening, finely slice salami which has been coated with chilli. Pop it under the griller until it crisps. Crumble it onto the cold mixture along with some grated tasty cheese. Mix it together, then follow the procedure for assembling and cooking a curry puff (page 124).

No. 17

Warm a little olive oil in a pan, add some diced onion and thin slivers of raw ginger and garlic. Add roughly chopped asparagus flowerets. Peel the course tough skin from the asparagus stalks, chop them finely and add to the pan. Sprinkle lightly with garlic salt. Once the flowerets have softened (don't worry about the chopped stalks), remove the mixture from the pan and let it go cold.

While the asparagus is cooking, shred some eye fillet steak after removing all the fat and sinews. Shredding the steak is easily achieved with a sharp knife. Simply hold the knife upright on the fillet and vigorously rub it back and forth. Combine the raw meat with the asparagus mixture. Place it on half a circle of puff pastry and sprinkle the full circle with Parmesan cheese, then follow the procedure for assembling and cooking a curry puff (page 124).

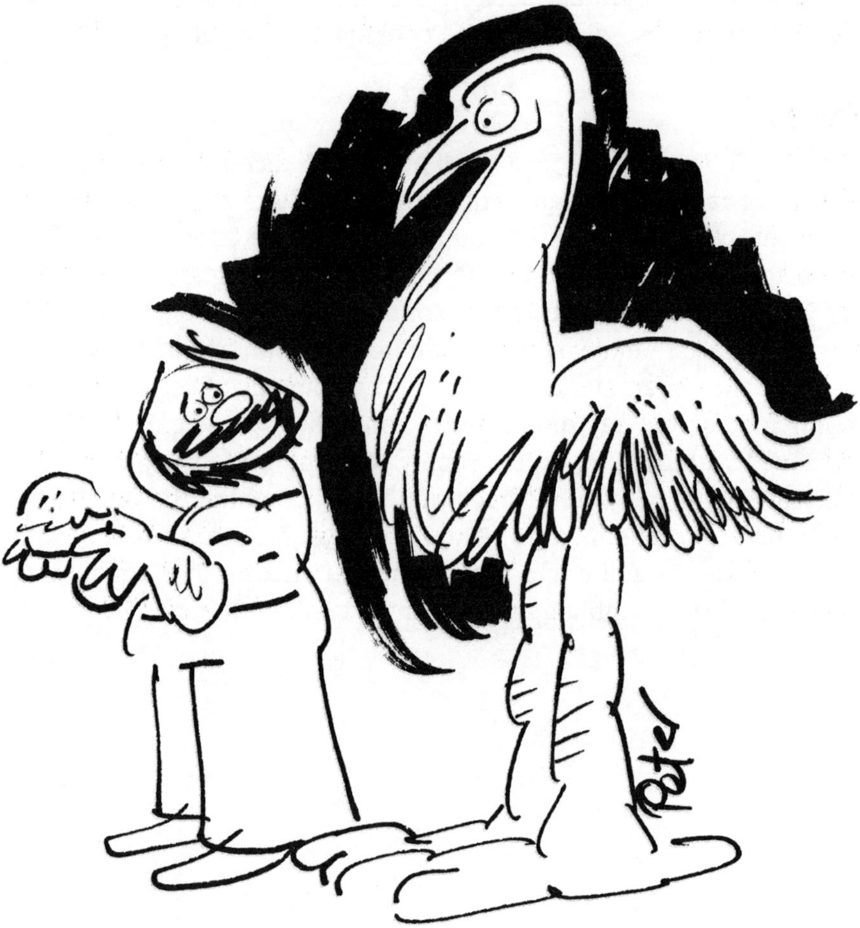

Festive pies

Emu pie

Emus are all right as long as you don't have an altercation with them. Under normal circumstances, they're quite happy to leave you alone provided you return the courtesy. Although I have known the odd emu to be a trifle curious.

Timber Town, just out of Port Macquarie, supported a resident emu whose hunger was unquenchable. Visitors to the historical town of timber cutters were unceremoniously deprived of their Timber Town burger by a quick, determined snap of the emu's strong beak as it leaned over a shoulder to snatch its morning or afternoon tea. And it was no good trying to hide your food in trouser pockets or carry bags because the emu with its long, rubbery neck had no intention of allowing you to do so. The bird's persistence usually won the day and the visitor would throw the food in the air and frantically beat a retreat.

But now we humans are able to get our own back on the birds — we're eating them.

Many fine Australians cannot bring themselves to eat an emu. 'Golly gosh,' they groan. 'They're part of our coat of arms and should be protected.'

Others say we eat all sorts of animals so why not the emu because, after all, they are in plague proportions. Some farmers

Emu pie

have no end of trouble and so, rather sensibly, they've turned to farming the big birds. And instead of the farmer making a loss, he not only puts a penny in his own pocket but helps Australia's export income as well.

Anyway, a short time ago, my mates at the bank descended on me for lunch. Pulling the pies from the oven I fed my visitors with ease and grace — or I should say ease and emus because, no doubt you have guessed, the pastry parcels were fleshed with Australia's feathered but flightless Big Bird.

After they'd eaten every skerrick and commented that 'You can't beat beef', I told them it was emu.

I thought that might ruffle a few feathers but, in fact, no one fainted and I did get a request for this recipe.

FESTIVE PIES

Individual emu pie

Ingredients

splash olive oil

½ large brown onion, diced

1 garlic clove, peeled and minced

splash soy of sauce

good pinch of dried oregano

good pinch of dried rosemary

125–185 g (4–6 oz) emu meat

splash of red wine

coarsely cracked black pepper

½ cup mixed, softened lima beans, chick peas and black-eyed beans

¾ cup mashed potato

1 sheet ready-made puff pastry

1 egg, beaten

poppyseeds

Method

Soften the onion and garlic in olive oil. Add the soy sauce and crumble in the oregano and rosemary.

Finely cut the emu meat into coarse mince. I don't grind meat as the process, in my opinion, squeezes the moisture from the flesh. I use a sharp knife and a little patience. Add a good handful of mince to the pan followed by a good splash of red wine. Add the black pepper and the mixed beans.

Turn the heat off and turn the mixture over in the hot pan because you only need to brown the meat.

Pop the mixture into an appropriately sized pie dish and put it in the fridge for 6–8 hours or overnight. The flavours will mingle with each other. Turn the mixture over a few times, to ensure it benefits from the moisture which gathers at the bottom of the pie dish.

When you are ready to proceed, ensure the mixture is moist, then drain off the excess moisture into a jar to be kept for another day. (As the base for a spaghetti sauce maybe.)

Coat the top of the mixture with 0.5–1 cm (¼–½") layer of mashed potato. On top of this layer, place a pie dish →

FESTIVE PIES

shaped piece of puff pastry. Crimp the edges and decorate the centre with flowers made from the off-cuts of the pastry.

Brush with beaten egg, sprinkle with poppyseed and pop into a pre-heated hot oven at 230°C (450°F) for 25 minutes.

Pâté of goose or duck with a crust

Ingredients

a duck or goose, or 1 kg (2 lb) poultry pieces

salt

freshly ground black pepper

tarragon

1 quantity puff pastry (see page 10)

Method

Use your store-bought poultry pieces or draw and dress a young goose or duck. (Cut the bird in pieces taking care to joint it well and not to break the bones.) Put the pieces in a dish and let them marinate for about 10 hours with strong seasoning of salt, peppers and tarragon.

Make a lightly puffed pastry and leave it to rest for 10 minutes or so. Roll it out to the thickness of half a finger.

Arrange the pieces of poultry in a casserole dish or on a baking dish. Cover them with pastry into the form of a dome.

Put into a hot oven at 230°C (450°F), taking care to put the dish on a brick so that it does not touch the bottom of the oven. Let it cook gently for at least a good hour. When the crust is a good golden brown, protect the pastry with a buttered paper so that it does not burn and continue cooking. Serve hot.

FESTIVE PIES

Crusted turkey pie Serves 4–6

Ingredients

175 g (6 oz) butter

5 tablespoons plain flour

2½ cups chicken stock

1¼ cups cream

½ cup dry white wine

¾ cup grated tasty cheese

250 g (8 oz) mushrooms, sliced

250 g (8 oz) noodles

4 cups strips of cooked turkey

salt and pepper

extra ½ cup grated cheese

½ cup crushed cracker biscuits

Method

Melt half the butter in a saucepan, mix in the flour and gradually blend in the chicken stock, cream and wine. Cook over a low gas flame, stirring for 3 minutes after the mixture thickens and comes to the boil.

Stir in ½ cup cheese. Measure out 1 cup of sauce and blend the remaining cheese into this cup.

Melt the remaining butter in a pan, add the mushrooms and cook quickly, stirring until just softened. Drain.

Add the noodles slowly to some boiling, salted water and cook until just tender. Drain.

Combine the larger portion of sauce, the mushrooms, hot noodles and turkey strips. Add salt and pepper to taste.

Spoon into a large oiled casserole or individual ramekins. Spoon the 1 cup of sauce evenly over the surface and top with the combined extra cheese and biscuit crumbs.

Bake in the oven at 190°C (375°F) for about 25 minutes or until bubbling and lightly browned on top.

Rising sun

I accepted an invitation to be guest speaker at a Hoteliers' Association luncheon which was held in the upstairs room of the Rising Sun Hotel in South Melbourne.

A host of hoteliers turned up because Carlton & United turned on the grog and Orlando the wine. A bit like coals to Newcastle I thought as pot after pot was poured down into beer barrelled bellies.

My task was to talk about what I considered to be the best pub food.

'Pies,' I said. The public bar would serve a lesser pie, then the saloon bar, and the restaurant would offer the very best pies possible. This allows the publican to make his catering more efficient.

If one didn't want to employ chefs, the pies could be made off the premises in someone else's kitchen. Serving is made much easier and, as long as there is an interesting variety of pies, everybody would be happy.

I don't believe I convinced anybody that my theory had merit, as plates of sausages, gravy and mashed potatoes peppered the tables of my publican audience.

'If you're having a pint or two, mixed grill, chicken parmigiana is what people want, pal,' I was told, 'not pies.'

Nevertheless I recounted my story of the time when I attempted to introduce my pie philosophy into a restaurant which I co-owned with a well-known media personality. The restaurant was in the heart of the city and was quite salubrious.

'So will our pies be,' I insisted to my partner. 'Pigeon pie with red wine sauce. Snapper and béchamel sauce pie. Smoked salmon with Spanish onions and caper sauce pie. We can have oyster pie, or caviar pie if we wish.'

'You mean the pie's the limit,' sneered my friend.

Rising sun

Like many arguments, I didn't win this one. My media mate insisted on a conventional menu, I still plugged for pies, and so we parted. The restaurant eventually went belly up because of bad management. I, of course, insist that the demise was due to the pie being passed over.

Pigeon pie (from Queen Victoria's Chef) Serves 6

Ingredients

6 young pigeons or squabs

12 pigeon livers, or if unavailable, use chicken livers

3 tablespoons chopped parsley

6 dobs butter

salt

freshly ground black pepper

6 rather large thin slices of beef, rump or fillet

1 cup mushrooms

8 hard-boiled egg yolks

sauce (see Method)

1 quantity puff pastry (see page 10)

Method

Draw, truss and singe six young pigeons; then stuff them with the chopped pigeon livers, mixed with some parsley, a small piece of butter, pepper and salt. Next, cover the bottom of the dish with rather large slices of beef, taken either from the fillet or rump; season with chopped parsley and mushrooms, pepper and salt; over these place the pigeons and between each pigeon put the yolk of an egg boiled hard, placing two or three in the centre also; add some white or brown sauce, whichever may be at hand, in sufficient quantity to produce sauce enough for the dish, or if neither of these be ready, then substitute some gravy or common broth; repeat the seasoning, cover the pie with puff pastry, bake it for an hour and a half and send to table.

FESTIVE PIES

Quail and caviar tarts Serves 6

Ingredients

315 g (10 oz) ready-made puff pastry

12 quail eggs less 1 teaspoon of white from each egg

1 small tin caviar

Method

Line 12 × 7 cm (3") tart moulds with the pastry. Break the quail eggs—one per tart.

Bake in the oven at 200°C (400°F) for 10 minutes.

Cool and place a fine line of caviar round the edge of each tart.

Sweet pies

Pear pie Serves 8–10

Ingredients

6 large pears

½ cup sugar

½ quantity puff pastry (see page 10)

1 egg yolk, beaten

Method

Peel and core the pears and cut them into thin slices. Pile the pear slices in the shape of a pyramid in a deep 20 cm (8") pie plate and sprinkle them with sugar.

Roll out a 23 cm (9") round of puff pastry to the thickness of 3 mm (⅛") and cover the pears with it, taking care not to pull the pastry. Wet the rim of the pie plate and the under edge of the pastry and pinch them together.

Brush with the egg yolk. Make a few slashes in the pastry with the point of a knife.

Bake in the oven at 220°C (425°F) for about 25 minutes. Serve with cream and/or ice-cream.

SWEET PIES

Mince pie

Pastry

Ingredients

5 heaped tablespoons flour

60 g (2 oz) butter

6 tablespoons milk

3 tablespoons water

Method

Put the flour into a bowl, and rub in the butter until it looks like breadcrumbs. Slowly mix in the milk and then the water, drawing the flour and butter into the liquid until you have a pliable dough. Roll out the dough to fit the top of your terrine.

Filling

Ingredients

3–5 cups seasonal fruit

½ handful of gooseberries

1 cup sugar

250 g (8 oz) butter

cinnamon, nutmeg or ginger

Method

In the bottom of a terrine put a layer of butter knobs, then a bed of a fruit in season: apples, pears, plums, apricots, peaches, sticks of rhubarb, cut in pieces. Add gooseberries, a layer of sugar, a layer of butter knobs, and so on until the terrine is full.

Add some cinnamon or nutmeg or ginger according to the fruit used. Cover with tart pastry, sealing the edges of the terrine well.

Place terrine in a pan filled with water and put it in a gentle oven 190°C (375°F) with buttered paper on top. Cook for approximately 30 minutes.

SWEET PIES

Jackson pie Serves 10–12

Ingredients

½ quantity sweet shortcrust pastry (see page 9)

6 tablespoons butter

¾ cup sugar

½ cup plain flour

¼ cup Marsala

1 egg

1 teaspoon vanilla

⅔ cup chopped walnuts

⅔ cup chocolate chips

vanilla ice-cream

Method

Blind bake the shortcrust pastry in a 23 cm (9") pie plate (see page 15).

Pop a baking tray on the middle rack of the oven and heat to 190°C (375°F).

Cream butter with sugar in a large bowl until fluffy. Blend in the flour. Add the Marsala, egg and vanilla and beat well. Stir in walnuts and chocolate chips.

Turn out into the pie crust. Cover edge of the pastry with foil to prevent excessive browning.

Put the pie onto the baking tray and bake for 45–50 minutes until the filling is lightly browned. Serve warm with ice-cream.

SWEET PIES

Glacé citrus pie Serves 10–12

Ingredients

½ quantity sweet shortcrust pastry (see page 9)

3 eggs

1 egg yolk

juice of 3 lemons, strained

juice of 1 orange, strained

150 ml (5 fl oz) cream

150 g (5 oz) caster sugar

6 very thin slices of glacé citron, chopped

6 pieces of glacé orange or lemon

3 glacé cumquats

Method

Line a 23 cm (9") pie tin with the pastry. Prick the bottom with a fork and bake for 10 minutes at 190°C (375°F).

While the pastry is cooking, whisk the eggs until light and fluffy. Add remaining ingredients except the glacé fruit.

Pour into the pastry case and decorate with the glacé fruit.

Bake until the filling is set, about 15–20 minutes. It should be a light golden colour. Serve warm or cold with cream.

SWEET PIES

Lime tart Serves 10–12

Ingredients

250 g (8 oz) plain flour

100 g (3 oz) icing sugar

pinch of salt

15 g (½ oz) unsalted butter

4 egg yolks

1 teaspoon vanilla essence

1 egg white, beaten

Syrup Ingredients

1 cup water

juice of 1 orange

½ cup sugar

a lime, thinly sliced

Filling Ingredients

2 eggs plus 1 extra yolk

juice and zest of a lemon, lime and orange

150 g (5 oz) icing sugar

75 g (2½ oz) unsalted butter, melted

Method

Sift the flour, sugar and salt into a food processor. Cut the butter into small pieces and combine with the dry ingredients, turning the processor on and off.

Whisk the vanilla into the yolks and pour into the processor. Continue to process until the mixture 'balls'.

Wrap the dough in plastic and chill. It is a very light pastry and is very soft, so it will need to be firm before you roll it.

Roll out pastry to fit a 23 cm (9") tart tin. Prick the base thoroughly and chill for an hour.

Bake at 180°C (350°F) for 10–12 minutes. Remove from the oven and brush with the beaten egg white. Continue to cook until light golden (about 5 minutes). The egg white prevents the base becoming soggy.

Make a syrup with the water, orange juice and sugar by putting them into a pan and bringing to the boil. Simmer the lime slices in the syrup until translucent and almost toffee-like. Do this very slowly to avoid damaging the flesh. Drain on a wire rack to cool.

To make the filling, beat the eggs and extra yolk with the zest and sugar until it forms a ribbon. →

SWEET PIES

Pour on the juices and melted butter and mix well. Pour the filling into the prebaked crust and place in the oven.

Cook at 180°C (350°F) for 20–30 minutes. The mixture should be firm but still 'wobbly'. It will set as it cools.

When cool, arrange the lime slices on top and glaze the top with some syrup. Serve with a little lightly whipped cream.

Lemon cream cheese pie Serves 10–12

Ingredients

250 g (8 oz) cream cheese

440 g (14 oz) sweetened condensed milk

3 eggs, separated

2 teaspoons grated lemon rind

¼ cup lemon juice

1 × 23 cm (9") fluted sponge flan

2 tablespoons orange juice

½ cup caster sugar

flaked almonds

Method

Beat cream cheese until smooth. Add the condensed milk, egg yolks, lemon rind and lemon juice. Mix well.

Place sponge flan onto a baking tray. Pour the orange juice over the flan, then pour in the cream cheese mixture.

Beat egg whites until soft peaks form then gradually beat in the sugar until stiff peaks form.

Place large spoonsful of meringue around the edge of the lemon filling forming a circle.

Sprinkle with almonds.

Bake at 180°C (350°F) for 10–15 minutes, lightly browning meringue.

SWEET PIES

Pecan pie Serves 10–12

Ingredients

½ *quantity sweet shortcrust pastry (see page 9)*

3 eggs

⅔ cup dark corn syrup

2 tablespoons butter, melted

⅔ cup sugar

1 cup pecan halves

Method

Line a 23 cm (9") pie dish with the pastry, then pop it into the freezer for 10 minutes.

Combine the remaining ingredients except the pecans and beat them until the mixture is smooth. Stir in the pecans.

Pour the mixture into the chilled pie shell (the pecans will rise to the top).

Bake at 190°C (375°F) for about 50 minutes until the filling is set and the pastry crisp and golden. Cool. Serve topped with whipped cream or ice-cream.

Custard tarts Serves 8

Ingredients

4 sheets ready-made puff pastry

1 or 2 egg whites

2 eggs, beaten

¾ cup sugar

dash of almond extract

1½ cups milk (heated to steaming)

Method

Cut rolled pastry into 9 cm (4") circles. Line the inside of 8 muffin cups with the pastry. Brush the bottoms with the unbeaten egg white, then pop them into the freezer for 5 minutes to chill.

Combine the 2 eggs with the sugar, almond extract and heated milk.

Pour the mixture into the chilled shells and bake in the oven at 200°C (400°F) for about 20 minutes, until the top of the custard is glazed and browned and the pastry is golden.

Put them straight into the fridge to chil but when they're set take them out. Serve at room temperature.

SWEET PIES

Rhubarb pie Serves 10–12

Ingredients

1 quantity sweet shortcrust pastry (see page 9)

5 cups diced rhubarb

1¼ cups sugar

3 tablespoons tapioca

¼ cup water

pinch of salt

1 tablespoon butter

Method

Line a 23 cm (9") pie dish with pastry. Fill with the diced rhubarb.

Combine the sugar, tapioca, water and salt. Let stand for 5 minutes, then spoon it over the rhubarb. Dot with butter.

Brush the edges of the pastry with water and put on a pastry lid, pressing well down to seal.

Bake in oven at 200°C (400°F) for 40 minutes or until the pastry is golden and crisp.

Old-fashioned apple pie Serves 8

Ingredients

6 large Granny Smith apples, peeled, cored and thinly sliced

125 g (4 oz) sugar

¼ teaspoon each ground cinnamon and nutmeg

6 whole cloves

1 teaspoon grated lemon rind

1 tablespoon lemon juice

1½ tablespoons butter

1 quantity shortcrust pastry (see page 9)

1 egg, beaten

Method

Mix all the ingredients together (except the pastry and egg).

Line a deep pie dish with the pastry. Spoon in the filling, then cover with a layer of pastry. Decorate the edges with a fork or by pinching the pastry between thumb and forefinger to make little 'waves'.

Pop a pastry rose or apple shape with leaves on top of the pie. Brush with beaten egg and bake in the oven at 180°C (350°F) for about an hour or until the pastry is a golden brown.

The last crust

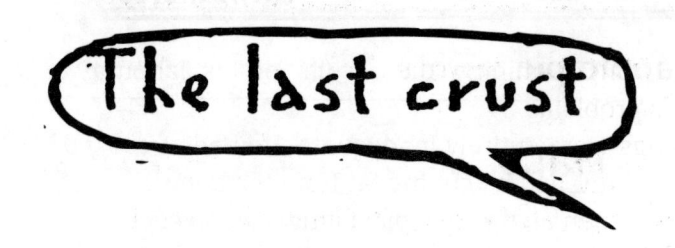

The last crust has been broken through and the filling that it protected finished. The ovens have been switched off and the Everest pile of dirty pie dishes is about to be tackled.

The kitchen staff organised by my wife, Jan, are demanding a slap-up, sit-down meal to celebrate the final recipe being put to print. And I'm feeling a bit half-baked as it was great fun recalling the laughter and tears which punctuated the part of my life, and those of my family and friends, that had been devoted to pies.

Now I have to contemplate a relatively normal life.

Oh, the pies will still play an important part of the future but the frantic race to keep pace with printing deadlines and the prying into pals' kitchens to pinch the odd idea — hang on — what am I talking about? I'll probably still pinch recipes from my pals and, if the truth be known, nothing at all will alter. In fact, now I really come to think of it, I hope it doesn't.

There'll be another book but with the focus on different food, though it'll still be good fun.

So that's about it. But, oh, just before I close the oven door on these pages, there is one story I didn't tell you.

A psychologist mate of mine phoned to ask me to cook osso buco for him.

'Actually,' he admitted, 'I've cooked it but it's not that good so I thought you may be able to help me, as I've asked my boss and his wife over for dinner.'

'When?' I asked.

'Tonight,' he replied.

'That's now!' I squealed. 'Look at the time. Don't throw out what you've already cooked, and I'll be right over.'

The last crust

I fled there and, on examining the results of his labours, I explained to him his problems.

One, his flavourings were entirely inadequate. He hadn't cooked the flesh long enough, nor had he cut the fat from the bones.

I picked up the saucepan *et al* and popped it into the freezer.

'Strewth, mate. What are you doing?' he spluttered.

'Fear not, lad,' I encouraged him.

Within fifteen minutes I was able to take the cold fat from the top of the saucepan where it had become solid.

'Right. That's one job done. Now we correct the seasoning. Job two done.'

I then cut all the flesh from the bones, scraped out the marrow, put the lot into a pie dish with a good squeeze of lemon juice and then grated the zest of lemon over the lot. For good luck and added heat, I also grated some fresh ginger into the mixture. I added slivers of black olives, capped the lot with puff pastry, brushed it with beaten egg and popped it into a hot oven. (By now, dear reader, you know the temperatures off by heart.)

'What'll I do with the mashed potatoes, mate?' he asked.

'Mix butter into them,' I instructed as I grated a fine looking carrot and then a parsnip. I quickly sautéed those in a pan with a touch of olive oil and the juice of a couple of garlic cloves. I then had my friend stir those into his creamed potatoes while I made up a crisp green side-salad.

The employer and his formidable wife arrived, the formalities were conducted, the accepted alcohol dispensed, then all were seated at a table bedecked with fresh flowers and candles in arty wrought iron.

Fish balls sprinkled with Chinese Five Spices were wrapped in spring roll pastry which had been liberally sprinkled on the inside with grated tasty cheese, then crisped in oil and served alongside a Thai sauce.

Soup made with beetroot and chicken stock followed, then this was trumped by the osso buco pie.

I must tell you, dear reader, that that osso buco pie was one of the great taste sensations I have experienced. The full flavour of the veal, mixed and married with the vegetables and spices which

The last crust

were heightened by the lemon, made a magnificent meal.

The softened potatoes and their additions allowed the juices of the serving of pie to be swept up, while the salad added a crispness and freshness to the adventure.

The dessert was fresh fruits sprinkled with pepper and wet with a mixture of juices and alcohol.

My friend was ecstatic and his guests left in ecstasy as I leave you dear reader.

Thank you.

PETER RUSSELL-CLARKE